D0616807

AQUATIC TYPES
& Others
Who Want to
Make a Splash

VGM Careers for You Series

CAREERS FOR

AQUATIC TYPES

& Others
Who Want to
Make a Splash

Blythe Camenson

VGM Career Horizons
NTC/Contemporary Publishing Group

Library of Congress Cataloging-in-Publication Data

Camenson, Blythe.
  Careers for aquatic types & others who want to make a splash / Blythe
Camenson.
      p.   cm. — (VGM careers for you series)
      ISBN 0-658-00215-5 (c). — ISBN 0-658-00216-3 (p)
      1. Vocational guidance—United States. I. Series.
  HF5382.5.U5C2515   1999
  331.7′02—dc21   99–29187
                                                                    CIP

Published by VGM Career Horizons
A division of NTC/Contemporary Publishing Group, Inc.
4255 West Touhy Avenue, Lincolnwood (Chicago), Illinois 60712-1975 U.S.A.
Copyright © 2000 by NTC/Contemporary Publishing Group, Inc.
Printed in the United States of America
International Standard Book Number: 0-658-00215-5 (cloth)
                                    0-658-00216-3 (paper)
 00 01 02 03 04 05 LB 18 17 16 15 14 13 12 11 10 9 8 7 6 5 4 3 2 1

Contents

Acknowledgments

The author would like to thank the following professionals for providing information about their aquatic careers:

STEVEN BAILEY, Curator of Fishes, New England Aquarium

CLAIRE BEST, Swimming Instructor

DAVID BUTTS, Deputy Public Affairs Officer, U.S. Navy

BEVERLEY CITRON, Assistant Cruise Director

RANDY JUSTICE, National Park Ranger

ROSE ELIZABETH LEDBETTER, Lifeguard

THOMAS MACPHERSON, Chief Engineer

JENNY MONTAGUE, Assistant Curator, Marine Mammals, New England Aquarium

WOODY POITIER, Paramedic/Firefighter

JAMES ROMAN STILIPEC, Journalist, U.S. Navy

RICHARD TURNWALD, Cruise Ship Purser

HEATHER URQUHART, Senior Aquarist, New England Aquarium

LEE WOODS, Charter Skipper and Sailing Instructor

CHAPTER ONE

Scanning the Horizon

An Overview

D oes the idea of working in an office building give you claustrophobia? Are you a sun, sky, and surf type of person? If so, then *Careers for Aquatic Types & Others Who Want to Make a Splash* will give you an ocean of opportunities to elude the land and embrace the sea. From lifeguarding to studying the ocean floor, to training marine mammals or entertaining guests aboard a cruise ship, you'll be able to find your sea legs within the following pages.

Choosing Your Field

People who work in and around the water give of themselves in many different capacities, providing valuable services—and having fun. If you're reading this book, chances are you're already considering a career in one of the many areas of this wide-open category. But perhaps you're not sure of the working conditions that different fields offer or which area would suit your personality, skills, and lifestyle the most. There are several factors to consider when deciding which sector to pursue. Each field carries with it different levels of responsibility and commitment. To identify occupations that will match your expectations, you need to know what each job entails.

Ask yourself the following questions and make note of your answers. Then, as you read through the next seven chapters, compare your requirements to the information you're provided with. In many of the chapters you will also read firsthand accounts from people working in the field. Their comments will help you pinpoint the fields that would interest you and eliminate those that would clearly be the wrong choice. What better way to learn about a career than from someone already established and experienced in that particular field?

- How much time are you willing to commit to training? Some skills can be learned on the job or in a year or two of formal training; others can take considerably longer.

- Do you want to work on land or at sea? Should your job make sure you are free of a desk and all the other office-type accoutrements?

- Can you handle a certain amount of stress on the job, or would you prefer a quiet—and safe—environment?

- How much money do you expect to earn starting out and after you have a few years' experience under your belt? Salaries and earnings vary greatly in each profession.

- How much independence do you require? Do you want to be your own boss, or will you be content as a salaried employee?

- Would you rather work daytime hours, or would you prefer evenings or weekends?

Knowing what your expectations are, then comparing them to the realities of the work will help you make informed choices.

Your Aquatic Options

In this book we cover a variety of job options, but the list is by no means exhaustive. As you do your own research and investigate how you might combine your love of the water with a satisfying career, you will, no doubt, uncover others.

Here are several to get you started. You can read more about these careers—and others—in the pages ahead.

- *Aquatic science* is the general term for research conducted in oceans and coastal or inland waters connected to the sea. Under this broad category fall oceanographers, marine mammal experts, geologists, and archaeologists, to name a few.

- *Navy and Coast Guard* careers provide good opportunities for aquatic types. From patrolling inland waters for the Coast Guard to working as a journalist for the U.S. Navy, you can find a place to put your skills to good use.

- *Commercial fishing* lends itself to strenuous work, long hours, and seasonal jobs. But for those who prefer to combine their love of the sea with a need for independence, this field might be the one for them. The proportion of self-employed workers in this field is among the highest in the economy.

- *Water transportation* workers operate and maintain all sorts of seagoing vessels, including tugboats, cargo ships, and ferries. The career options, from captain to mechanic, are broad and plentiful.

- *Cruise Staff* work can be fun and exciting, with the opportunity to travel to exotic ports and meet different kinds of people. Jobs run the gamut from purser to activities director.

- *Water Safety* offers a wide range of employment opportunities, from lifeguarding at summer camps to rescue duties working for the National Park Service.

- *Water Sports* work can let you pass on your skills to others while you enjoy the sun and surf. Adult education programs, summer camps, the Red Cross, YMCAs, private resorts, and a variety of other organizations regularly employ instructors to teach swimming, sailing, and all the other water activities.

The Training You'll Need

The training required for the different aquatic careers varies greatly. Some positions are entry level, requiring no more than a high school education. Others demand you be physically fit and have some prior work experience. Others require specific skills and a college degree—some even require postgraduate training at the Ph.D. level.

Salaries

Just as the training you'll need for aquatic occupations varies greatly, so do the salaries. In general, the more education and training required for a position, the more you'll earn. But that isn't always the case. Other factors also determine salaries, such as the geographic region in which you work and the size and the budget of the hiring organization. In each chapter ahead you'll learn the different salaries for each occupation.

For More Information

In the Appendix you will find professional associations for many of the career paths explored in this book. Most offer booklets and pamphlets with career information; some are free, and others might have a nominal charge of one or two dollars. Most organizations will respond to your letter within a few days.

CHAPTER TWO

Aquatic Scientists

S o you want to work with dolphins or whales? In this chapter you'll learn how to go about it. But aquatic science offers much more than just working with marine mammals. Aquatic science can be categorized as a subfield under botany (the study of aquatic plant forms) or zoology (the study of aquatic animals). It encompasses several fields and career paths—in fact, many universities offer separate programs or departments in the various aspects of aquatic science. Let's take a look at the options.

Aquatic Science

Aquatic scientists study virtually everything having to do with water. For example, *aquatic chemists* research organic, inorganic, and trace-metal chemistry. *Marine geologists* study how ocean basins were formed and how geothermal and other geological processes interact with seawater. *Freshwater geologists* may study past climates or the organisms found in the sediments.

Aquatic scientists could also study processes that cover time scales ranging from less than a second to millions of years. They may also examine activity in spaces ranging from millimeters to ocean-wide.

Aquatic science is interdisciplinary. While most aquatic scientists generally specialize in just one area, they use information from all fields and often work together with other related scientists in teams. For example, chemists and biologists might work together to understand the ways in which the chemical components of water bodies interact with plants, animals, and microorganisms such as bacteria.

Oceanography

Oceanography is the specific study of the biological, chemical, geological, optical, and physical characteristics of oceans and estuaries. The subfields of oceanography are physical oceanography, chemical oceanography, biological oceanography, and geological and geophysical oceanography.

Physical oceanographers study currents, waves, and motion and the interaction of light, radar, heat, sound, and wind with the sea. They are also interested in the interaction between the ocean and atmosphere and the relationship between the sea, weather, and climate.

Chemical oceanographers study chemical compounds and the many chemical interactions that occur in the ocean and on the ocean floor.

Biological oceanographers are interested in describing the diverse life-forms in the sea, their population densities, and their natural environments. They try to understand how these animals and plants exist in interrelationships with other sea life and substances and also focus on the impact of human intervention on the oceanic environment.

Geological and *geophysical oceanographers* study the shape and nature and origin of the material of the seafloor.

Oceanographer is a term that is usually understood to include ocean scientists, ocean engineers, and ocean technicians.

Ocean scientists investigate how the oceans work. They usually have graduate degrees in oceanography with bachelor's degreesin one of the fundamental science fields such as biology, physics, chemistry, or geology.

Ocean engineers perform the usual tasks of any engineers—such as designing a structure—but they deal with specific issues related to that structure and its environment in the sea. For example, an ocean engineer might design supports for oil well drilling equipment that would stand on the ocean floor. They would have to take into account all information about ocean currents and the force they would exert on the structure, plus saltwater corrosion, marine life interference, and other similar elements. Ocean engineers also design the equipment oceanographers use to make oceanographic measurements.

Ocean technicians are responsible for equipment calibration and preparation, measurements and sampling at sea, instrument maintenance and repair, and data processing. Ocean technicians usually have bachelor's degrees, although some may be successful at finding work with two-year associate's degrees.

Marine Biology or Science

Marine biology or science refers specifically to the sea—saltwater environments—and covers a surprisingly wide variety of disciplines. Examples include planetology, meteorology, physics, chemistry, geology, physical oceanography, paleontology, and biology. Marine science also includes archaeology, anthropology, sociology, engineering, and other studies of human relationships with the sea.

Limnology

Limnology involves the same concerns as oceanography, but is limited to inland systems such as lakes, rivers, streams, ponds, and wetlands and includes both freshwater and salt water.

Physical limnologists study water movements while *optical limnologists* study the transmission of light through the water.

Marine Mammal Science

Marine mammal science (yes, the study of dolphins and whales) covers about a hundred species of aquatic or marine mammals that depend on freshwater or the ocean for part or all of their life. The species include pinnipeds, which covers seals, sea lions, fur seals, and walrus; cetaceans, which include baleen and toothed whales, ocean and river dolphins, and porpoises; sirenians, which covers manatees and dugongs; and some carnivores, such as sea otters and polar bears.

Marine mammal scientists work to understand these animals' genetic, systematic, and evolutionary relationships; population structures; community dynamics; anatomy and physiology; behavior and sensory abilities; parasites and diseases; and geographic and microhabitat distributions. Marine mammal scientists also study ecology, management, and conservation.

Archaeology

Archaeology is a subfield of anthropology. Archaeologists study the artifacts of past cultures to learn about history, customs, and living habits. They study the research of other archaeologists and survey and excavate archeological sites, recording and cataloging their finds. By careful analysis, archaeologists reconstruct earlier cultures and determine their influences on the present.

There are two subfields of archaeology that would be of particular interest to aquatic types:

Nautical archaeology is the study of shipwreck sites, either on land or underwater.

Underwater archaeology is the study and excavation of submerged sites. Usually these are shipwrecks, but underwater archaeology includes the study of submerged habitation sites as well.

Employers of Aquatic Scientists

Aquatic scientists find employment in universities and colleges. They also work for international organizations, federal and state agencies, private companies, nonprofit laboratories, local governments, or aquariums, zoos, marine parks, or museums. They also may be self-employed.

Government agencies that hire aquatic scientists include:

Army Corps of Engineers

Coast Guard

Department of Commerce

Department of Energy

Department of the Interior

Department of the Navy

Department of State

Environmental Protection Agency

Marine Mammal Commission

Minerals Management Service

National Aeronautics and Space Administration

National Marine Fisheries Service

National Oceanic and Atmospheric Administration

National Park Service

National Science Foundation

Naval Oceanographic Office

Naval Research Laboratory

Office of Naval Research

Smithsonian Institution

U.S. Fish and Wildlife Service

U.S. National Biological Service

U.S. Navy, Office of Naval Research

However, the government is not the only place, by far, where aquatic scientists find employment.

Private industries—such as commercial fishing and oil and gas exploration, production, and transportation—hire aquatic scientists when their operations affect marine mammals or produce environmental concerns.

Many environmental, advocacy, and animal welfare organizations as well as legal firms also depend on aquatic scientists and use them for legal or policy development, problem solving, and regulatory and administrative roles.

Aquariums, marine parks, and zoos hire specialists for veterinary care, husbandry, training, research, and education programs. Examples of marine mammal jobs include researcher, field biologist, fishery vessel observer, laboratory technician, animal trainer, animal care specialist, veterinarian, whale-watch guide, naturalist, and educator.

Museums hire specialists for educational programs, research, and curatorial positions.

Magazines, book publishers, television, and radio also provide employment for specialists, but usually on a part-time freelance or consulting basis.

Later in this chapter you will find a close-up look at aquarium work, along with several firsthand accounts from professionals employed in aquariums in different capacities.

What the Work Is Like

Many aquatic science researchers spend time each year engaged in field work, collecting data and samples in natural environments. The data are collected during research cruises on small or large vessels, and the amount of time at sea can last from one week to more than two months and involve a team of scientists from many disciplines.

Limnological data most often are collected during short, one- to two-day field trips that are usually narrower in scope. But, at the other extreme, trips can involve stays at field stations lasting from days to months.

When not in the field, aquatic research scientists spend most of their time in the laboratory running experiments or at the computer analyzing data or developing models. They also study papers in scientific journals and relate that research to their own work. Writing their own papers for publication is also part of their routine.

Those working in universities must couple lectures and student conferences with their own research. In any environment, attending meetings is also part of the job. Scientists may also spend time writing research proposals to obtain grant money for more research.

For aquatic scientists with administrative jobs, the time is spent in the office or communicating with colleagues and the public. Like any research scientists, they also attend national or international conferences to keep up in their fields.

Hands-on workers, such as those involved with marine mammals or working in aquariums, have jobs that are not as glamorous as movies or TV programs depict. The work involves hard labor, such as lugging buckets of fish and cleaning tanks.

Training for a Career in Aquatic Science

There are a few entry-level positions here and there for people with only high school diplomas, but these positions are rare and opportunities for career advancement are limited.

Most entry-level jobs require a bachelor's degree in a natural science from an accredited college or university. Because most bachelor degree programs do not usually require research experience, applicants may expect to participate as assistants in research and advance mostly on the basis of on-the-job experience.

A master's degree is required by many employers, especially where research is a large part of the job description. A doctorate is usually necessary for academic positions or in other settings where the employee would manage other scientists and conduct studies of his or her own design.

Job opportunities are varied and exist at all educational levels. As with other fields, the higher-level and better-paying jobs require the most education.

Because aquatic science encompasses so many specializations, at the undergraduate level it is advised that future biologists obtain the broadest education possible. There is no guarantee you will gain employment in your area of interest or specialization—at least not right away. Because of this, a general education will provide a foundation for many types of employment.

Aquatic scientists usually acquire a foundation in one or more of the basic sciences such as biology, chemistry, geology, mathematics, or physics before specializing.

Many of the disciplines in aquatic science, such as marine biology, are graduate-level pursuits, so when choosing your undergraduate program, it's a good idea to investigate the strengths and specializations of the biology programs. If you know you want to pursue graduate work in marine science, for example, then earning your undergraduate degree at a university that offers courses in that area will help when it comes time to apply to graduate school. But graduate schools prefer students to major in a core science such as biology, physics, chemistry, or geology rather than a specialized subject such as limnology or oceanography.

You can specialize in the areas that interest you the most, but not exclusively. Make sure to add statistics, mathematics, computers, and data management to your curriculum. And, as in any profession, good oral and writing skills are crucial.

To increase your employability, involvement in a research project in a science laboratory is also important. This might be pursued through your university as a supervised independent study, working with a particular professor's research project, or through an internship, work-study job, or a stint of volunteering. If your university doesn't offer opportunities in this area, seek out other aquatic scientists, perhaps working at a local aquarium or marine science center, and volunteer to help in any way you can.

In addition, many summer research programs are available at universities with graduate-level limnology or oceanography programs. These summer research experiences are usually offered to students after they have completed their sophomore or junior year and offer a good chance to learn more about the discipline as a possible career choice. You can find out about these programs by writing to institutions offering graduate degrees in limnology or oceanography. The programs are open to students from all universities.

To further prepare yourself, you can also attend seminars and join aquatic science organizations such as the American Society of Limnology and Oceanography. (The address is provided at the end of this chapter.) By doing so you will better understand the field and start making contacts in the community of people in which you'll eventually work.

Many careers in marine mammal science require additional qualifications such as scuba certification and boat-handling experience.

To summarize, make sure you acquire a well-rounded education and are familiar with what's happening in aquatic science. Get involved in projects, talk to scientists, and participate in any way you can.

Finding an Aquatic Science Program

Information on colleges and universities offering programs in aquatic science and all its subfields can be found through various directories such as Lovejoy's or Peterson's, available at school guidance centers, public libraries, or on the Internet. You will find the programs listed under various headings:

Aquatic Science

Biology

Chemistry

Earth Science

Geology

Limnology

Marine Biology

Marine Ecology

Meteorology

Ocean Engineering

Oceanography

Physics

Career Outlook

In general, opportunities are good for whose with a bachelor's degree or higher in science. But some specialty areas present stiff competition to job applicants. For example, there may be ten thousand people who want a job working with marine mammals, but there are only around a hundred jobs in this area nationwide. That is one extreme. In other specializations, there may be only five jobs nationwide but only four qualified applicants.

Generally speaking, there is more interest and, therefore, more competition for jobs in marine biology than there is in aquatic physics, chemistry, or geology.

Opportunities are best for those with training in mathematics or engineering and those who pursued an interdisciplinary program. Funding for graduate students and professional positions is expected to increase in the next ten years in the disciplines of global climate change, environmental research and management, fisheries science, and marine biomedical and pharmaceutical research programs. American students and scientists are also expected to become much more involved in international research programs.

Even when the number of available positions in this career path is small, top scientists are always in demand.

It is important to remember that job opportunities and openings in all fields change over time and can change quite quickly. If you follow your interests, work hard, make contacts, and don't give up, you'll find the job of your dreams.

Salaries

Aquatic scientists enter this field for the love of their work—not for the money. The salary you'll earn will depend in part on your educational background, experience, responsibilities, area of specialization, number of years of service, and the size, type, and geographical location of the employing institution. In general, jobs with the government or in industry have the highest pay.

Bachelor's degree holders with no experience may find employment with the federal government at GS-5 to GS-7 offers a salary range from the teens to the thirties. Doctorate degree holders generally earn from $30,000 to $80,000 per year and sometimes more than $100,000 per year as senior scientists or full professors. High competition in some areas will most likely keep salaries at a modest level.

Examples of aquatic sciences that presently pay above-average salaries are physical oceanography, marine technology and engineering, and computer modeling.

Some aquatic scientists earn their incomes from more than one source. They teach at universities, for example, then supplement their incomes by obtaining research grants from the federal or state government or private sources, writing for technical publications, and serving as consultants.

Salaries for Aquarists

Salaries vary depending upon the institution's funding and the size of its budget. An entry-level aquarist would start from the high teens to the low twenties. Senior aquarists would move up the ladder in the neighborhood of $27,000 to $30,000 a year. A supervisor could earn in the mid thirties to low forties.

Salaries for Trainers

Entry-level salaries begin in the twenties and go up from there. A trainer can advance quickly and, at the assistant curator level, earn between $30,000 and $45,000 depending upon experience.

Salaries for Curators

Salaries for curators range from the mid forties to the mid sixties, depending upon the number of years of accrued experience.

Job Titles Within Aquariums

The collections in large public aquariums require a variety of specialists to maintain them: engineers, accountants, animal trainers, curators, aquarists, and biologists. Other departments within aquariums are conservation, veterinarian services, design, research, education, marketing, and public relations. What follows is a sampling of typical jobs found in aquariums.

Aquarists

Aquarists are the frontline people who take care of the exhibits. One of the primary skills an aquarist must bring to the job is a nationally recognized certification as a scuba diver. In addition to maintaining and cleaning the exhibits, aquarists are the primary people responsible for stocking them. Depending on the size of the exhibit, an aquarist will do a lot of diving, both inside the exhibit tanks and collecting from local waters.

There are several aquarist rankings, and the job titles will vary depending upon the particular institution. In general they are aquarist-in-training, trained aquarist, senior aquarist, and supervisor.

At the New England Aquarium (profiled later in this chapter) aquarists are also divided into two main categories: diving aquarists and gallery aquarists. Diving aquarists dive into the large tank exhibit to maintain the health of the fish and to take care of the exhibit in general.

Gallery aquarists are in charge of smaller exhibits but many more of them. Gallery aquarists also spend time in the water, but they aren't in a wet suit everyday. Every aquarist gets wet; some get wet more often than others.

All aquarists go on collecting trips and use their diving skills in that capacity too. In addition, aquarists need fishing and boat-handling skills.

At some institutions, as aquarists become more experienced, they are given opportunties to develop their own special niches, getting involved in research or conservation projects as well as participating in collecting trips.

Curator

An aquarium's general curator takes care of all husbandry matters. Under this top position's jurisdiction would fall curators responsible for different areas of an aquarium's operation. For example, an aquarium could have curators of fishes, marine mammals, exhibit design, research, and conservation. These curator positions often involve more administrative than hands-on duties.

Trainer

At some institutions, trainers would follow rankings similar to aquarists: assistant trainer (or trainer-in-training), trainer, senior trainer, and supervisor. Trainers are responsible for the care of animals and the exhibits as well as teaching medical behaviors, presentation behaviors, and research behaviors. For more information, see the trainer's firsthand account later in this chapter.

Close-Ups

The following three people, who are providing firsthand accounts of their jobs, work in various positions at the New England Aquarium in Boston, Massachusetts. The New England Aquarium is one of the premiere showcases for the display of marine life and habitats. Its mission is to "present, promote, and protect the world of water." These goals are carried out through exhibits and through education, conservation, and research programs. Exhibits showcase the diversity, importance, and beauty of aquatic life and habitats and highlight aquatic conservation issues of importance.

The centerpiece for the aquarium is the 187,000-gallon Giant Ocean Tank Caribbean Coral Reef Exhibit, which rises through four stories of the facility. Visitors are afforded a multiangle view of sea turtles, sharks, moray eels, and the other tropical fish that live inside.

The Ocean Tray, which holds 131,000 gallons of water and surrounds the Giant Ocean Tank on the ground floor, is home to a colony of black-footed and rockhopper penguins.

In a floating pavilion adjacent to the aquarium, sea lion presentations of natural and learned behaviors are featured every day. Harbor seals reside in the outdoor pool on the aquarium's plaza. Some of these seals were found as orphaned pups along the New England coast and have been cared for by skilled aquarium biologists as part of their Rescue and Rehabilitation Program. Through this program, aquarium staff work with distressed or injured marine animals in the wild such as whales, dolphins, sea turtles, and seals. Their goals are to rescue, rehabilitate, and, whenever possible, release the animals back to the wild.

Other research programs include working to preserve the endangered red-bellied turtle species and to help increase the declining population of black-footed penguins. The New England Aquarium also offers a whale watch program and a "Science at Sea" harbor boat tour. To maintain such a range of exhibits and programs, the New England Aquarium relies on the skills and experience of a variety of professionals.

Steven Bailey, Curator of Fishes

Steven Bailey has been with the New England Aquarium since 1984. He received his bachelor's degree in zoology from Wilkes University in Wilkes-Barre, Pennsylvania, and completed substantial work toward a master's degree in ichthyology at Northeastern University in Boston. When a full-time job as an aquarist was offered to him at the aquarium, he jumped at the chance, moving up the ranks to his current position.

Steven Bailey's Background

"When I was in graduate school, I was planning for a job that would allow me to be paid to go diving. It was as simple as that. I definitely had an animal thing going and I had been diving since the sixties. My father, who is a forestry kind of guy, always outdoors, decided that my brother and I at a young age should know how to dive. I grew up in Pennsylvania but spent most of our summers diving at a lake in Maine. The perfect way to start.

"I spent four years in grad school and they were incredibly busy years, amassing experience to make me hirable. I volunteered with the National Marine Fishery Service, and on a number of occasions I spent time as a professional collector, collecting specimens that were used for biomedical research. I had a great deal of diving experience, and back in the early eighties there weren't a lot of folks around applying for these positions who had that experience. I was working seven days a week and going to school and just generally maximizing every minute. I heard about the job because I was volunteering here while I was going to graduate school. I had a mentor here, too, who recommended me.

"I started as an aquarist. Over a thirteen-year period I moved up the ranks, or should I say I moved out of the best job in the building to the most aggravating job. I spent ten years as an aquarist, then I got promoted to senior aquarist and somehow inexplicably bypassed that last supervisor step and went from senior aquarist to my present position as curator of fishes."

Steven Bailey's Responsibilities

"As curator of fishes, I am responsible for everything other than marine mammals—all the fishes, invertebrates, reptiles amphibians, birds, plants. My area involves the aquarium's two biggest exhibits, the Giant Ocean Tank, which is the centerpiece of the building, and the penguin colony, which is at the base of the tank.

"I am responsible for twenty-four people. There are nineteen aquarists at different levels and four supervisors, the equivalent of assistant curators. I also supervise a curatorial associate who keeps track of everything from how much frozen food we are feeding fishes to making sure all of our permits are up-to-date. She pitches in wherever she can, whether that's on a collecting trip or helping to haul a five-hundred-pound turtle out of an exhibit for a blood sampling.

"One of my duties is hiring. We can be incredibly selective about that. Every time there is a job opening advertised here, we receive at least two hundred resumes. We can be particular about the backgrounds that folks have. It must include diving, and it is up to them to make sure they have this training. They must also have a degree. Animal biology is preferred, but we also have people with environmental science or general biology degrees, too.

"People's work ethic is also very important; people who work hard to achieve a particular goal are very attractive to us. Sometimes you can see this on a resume. They want to be in contact with animals, so they'll do anything and everything to ensure that that happens, whether it's mucking out stalls, working for a vet, working in pet stores, or running their own grooming businesses. There are a lot of things people can do to be close to animals. Being interested in fishes is obviously a plus. Maybe someone has been a home hobbyist for years and can go on at length about the animals they've had in that time. Or maybe it is something they've developed more recently in life, as the result of a stimulating course they had in college. Some folks elect to do field experiences that are an epiphany to them. They manage to see something that they never thought of before and become quite enthralled with it.

"Primarily in this job I now deal with budget and personnel issues, or that's the way it seems. I am removed from the day-to-day hands-on work. If I had taken accounting courses and abnormal psychology, I would be much more prepared for this particular position than all the biology I studied.

"There are around eighty to ninety exhibits that come under my group's control. Those range in size from the 187,000-gallon Caribbean reef exhibit to a fifty-gallon sea horse and pipefish exhibit. Those exhibits need an incredible amount of scrutiny, from making sure the animals are nutritionally taken care of to the three Ws aspect of the aesthetics—the windows, the walls, the water. They all have to be clean and aesthetically appealing so that when folks come to visit us they are immediately assured that professionals are managing the animals. They spend money to visit here, and they should get a good return on their dollar. They are seeing the epitome of animal presentation, taking home a lot of good information, and getting a bit of an education while they're here.

"Aquariums and zoos in general have evolved in many ways to where they are stewards of the animals in the wild. The long-term survival of these animals hinges upon the successes of zoos and aquariums in general. What I mean by this is there are many animals that are endangered or threatened or enjoy some sort of status of special concern, and we are breeding facilities. We are restocking facilities for animals that are ready to go back into the wild to reestablish a population. There is no substitute for seeing the real thing. We can get an important message across, and this is an admirable and worthwhile job.

"Conservation and research and animal-breeding activities are all a big part of what zoos and aquaria are up to these days. We have an aquarist who spends a great deal of time in the Amazon each year. What he does is run an ecotourism operation where he has people paying to come on trips with him to assess biodiversity and explore the habitats of a number of these backwaters in the Amazon. The money generated from this is used to support Brazilian researchers who are doing things such as examining the ornamental fish industry. The most popular fish in the world as far as the home aquarist is concerned is a fish that comes out of the Rio Negro river system, a part of the Amazon River Basin. That animal is called the cardinal tetra. The cardinal tetra is single-handedly—or single-finnedly I suppose—responsible for the well-being of maybe forty to fifty thousand people who live on that river. They are all in some way a part of that industry. Because they exact a living from that sustainable fishery and are not in the forest slash-and-burn agriculturing or selling other animals' skins or parts, it is one of the most intact areas of the basin.

"I preferred it when I was able to get out in the field instead of being parked in front of a computer screen all day and attending lots and lots of meetings. The positive aspects of this job are much different than what initially attracted me to the field. I don't get out and go collecting that often, but I do manage to get a fair amount of satisfaction and sense of accomplishment from being involved in the design and exhibit construction end of things. We, as a group—the husbandry folks, the design department, education, research—get together to plot our course over the next few years.

"I am also married to someone who works here and is also an animal person, and life couldn't be better."

Advice from Steven Bailey

"It is a career for people who are very serious. There aren't that many opportunities, and you have to be really dedicated to this pursuit. Most of the folks here have not been hired right out of college. They spent a good deal of time volunteering at this institution and picking up a lot of other related work experiences, expanding their horizons, becoming very much Renaissance people. The diversity of experiences that individuals can have are very important as far as making them attractive commodities when the hiring time comes around. There are very few people here who were hired on their first go-round.

"This job requires that you have construction and tool skills. It demands you know your way around the literature or at least be able to find the information to answer a question or solve a problem. It requires an ability to be comfortable with routine and what can often become repetitive work.

"Being an aquatic chamber maid, which most everyone is, might sound like fun, but when you are cleaning and maintaining an animal's environment day after day, it can get very old for some people. For other people it's a Zen experience. They put it into perspective; they are able to be at peace with the incredible amount of responsibility they have for all of these animals.

"And not all of these animals have the excitement or energy that, say, a panda has or a killer whale. Those are animals that get a lot of attention from the public, but nevertheless an animal is an animal, and whether you are talking about a minnow that is abundant five miles away from this institution or one of those more glamourous animals, such as the California sea otter, the bottom line is still the same. They depend on you, and you are responsible for their well-being."

Heather Urquhart, Senior Aquarist

Heather Urquhart is a diving aquarist in the fishes department at the New England Aquarium in Boston. She is also a certified advanced scuba diver and has been working at the aquarium since 1989.

Heather Urquhart's Background

"I have always known that I wanted to work with animals. Early on I wasn't sure how, whether it would be veterinarian work or as a zookeeper. The opportunities I was aware of then for working with animals were limited. After I saw Jacques Cousteau, I knew I wanted to work with marine animals. I've always been an ocean buff; I grew up at the ocean. When I was a kid, I was always the one without a suntan. I always had my mask and snorkel on.

"I got a bachelor's degree in biology with a concentration in marine biology and a chemistry minor at Salem State College in 1985. Before I got my job here, I thought for sure I'd be going on for a master's, but once you get involved with your work doing something that you love, it's hard to break away to go back to school.

"Growing up in this area, I was always aware of the aquarium and what was going on. When I started school in Salem, which is very close to the city, I found out through friends at school about the aquarium's volunteer opportunities. While I was still in college, I volunteered here for six months, two days a week in 1984, coincidentally with the penguins, the area in which I am now working, . Also at the time we had river otters that we took care of. I was able to group all my classes on Monday, Wednesday, and Friday so I could volunteer Tuesday and Thursday.

"Once I graduated in 1985, I had a couple of other jobs—I worked with an environmental consulting firm for six months and did some quality-control work with seafood—but was constantly applying whenever a position came open here. I'd scan the newspapers and then send my resume in. It took a little while, but finally they brought me in for an interview, and, based on the good recommendations I had received as a volunteer and my interview, I got hired. That was in 1989, and I've been here ever since. I started as an aquarist-in-training then to aquarist then to my current title, senior aquarist. I am in the fishes department. Even though I work with the penguins, they are classified under the fishes department."

Heather Urquhart's Responsibilities

"I take care of both the Giant Ocean Tank and the penguin colony. I dive into the tank up to five times a day in order to feed and examine and check on the health of the fish as well as clean and maintain the exhibit. We have five dives going a day, so if we have enough people in, we'll rotate so sometimes we don't have to go in every day.

"The penguin exhibit has a 131,000-gallon tank, and we need seven staff people to maintain both exhibits, plus we have volunteers to help us seven days a week. We have forty-seven penguins right now. We don't have to dive in the penguin exhibit, but we do have to put on a wet suit to get in there. We are in fifty-five-degree water up to our chests. There are days you just don't feel like getting wet, but you just grin and bear it. If one of us is ill with a bad cold or the flu, then we try to accommodate each other, but even then I've gone in. There was no choice. The fish have to be fed.

"It's a very physical job, and it's not for everyone. Not only because you're in the water, but just the nature of putting on dive equipment and chugging down the hall to get into the tank, then pulling yourself out. Then, there's going up and down four flights of stairs in order to get to the penguin exhibit with fifteen pounds of fish in a bucket in each hand. There is an elevator, but it's a big freight elevator, and, by the time you get yourself in there and down, it's just easier to take the stairs. Besides that, you need a key to open the elevator, and when you're in a wet suit in salt water, you don't want to be carrying around metal keys. They corrode.

"Lately, my concentration has been with the penguins more. We don't do any training with the penguins; we want people to see them as they would be in the wild. We do have some penguins, though, that have been partially hand raised, and they tend to be more accustomed to human interaction. These penguins, we can take them out and do what we call an animal interview. They are put in an enclosure outside of the exhibit where visitors, without touching the animal, can still get an up-close-and-personal look. Some of our staff members will speak about the animal and give a presentation. While they aren't trained per se, these animals don't mind being in the spotlight. It's a joy to work with them.

"I enjoy the animal interactions the most; it's some of the best medicine going. No matter what kind of aggravating day you might be having, when you are working with the animals, it all seems not to matter so much.

"I've been here for quite a while, and I've hand raised a lot of little penguins, and that's a wonderful experience to be there from the egg to the adult stage. They imprint on you, and they know my voice and will come to me. We have them all banded, but I can recognize who's who. Once the hand-raised penguins mature a little and become interested in a mate, they tend to ignore us more. We are no longer as interesting to them.

"We keep a genealogy on all our penguins, and we keep food records and medical records and records of molting patterns. We also monitor their mating patterns to prevent inbreeding. If we notice a pair that would be a bad pair, we separate them and encourage them to breed with a penguin that would be a better match. In the wild you don't have that problem, but here we have to be careful. And with this particular species, we have to be careful because their numbers are so vulnerable in the wild right now.

"In addition to maintaining the exhibit, I've been lucky enough to form a conservation program surrounding our penguins. We house two species of penguins, rockhopper and the African penguin. The African penguins are on the verge of becoming an endangered species in the wild. Through the help of the aquarium, we've been able to set up a fund and generate monies here through a penny-smasher machine. It costs fifty-one cents—we keep the fifty cents, and the penny goes under a barrel that has the imprint of an African penguin on it. The penny gets smooshed with the logo on it, and the kids get a souvenir.

"In the past two years I've been to South Africa twice and intend to go again soon. We link up with conservation organizations there and join them with their conservation and research work, trying to contribute as much as we can, as well as bringing back the most factual data to the states to educate people about the penguins' plight. We are also educating ourselves. We want to be more than talking heads who have never been in the field. We also contribute to penguin rehabilitation organizations that are helping oiled penguins in South Africa. We have great hopes for the future—we are really moving and shaking with this thing. The past two years have been wonderful, a real windfall for me.

"We also do a lot of local travel up and down the East Coast for collecting fish and invertebrates for our exhibits. We also run a collecting trip twice a year down to the Bahamas to collect for our Caribbean reef exhibit. But we don't have to collect that much because we are pretty good at maintaining the exhibit.

"We have sharks in our Caribbean exhibit that we dive with, but they probably are what I worry about least in there. They are docile, and they don't pay much attention to us. I think people have a lot of misconceptions about sharks. People aren't on a shark's menu, and a lot of times attacks are the result of mistaken identity. In our tank we have some fish that are only about an inch or an inch and a half, yet they are much more aggressive than any shark. Little damselfish protecting their nests will come right out at you, for example. I've been bitten by damselfish on numerous occasions. We get our share of bites, not only from the fish, but from the penguins, too. They aren't trying to be mean, but you're down there feeding them and handling them, and they aren't tame animals. Most of the time it's our own mistakes. You're feeding a little piece of shrimp to a fish, and they miss the shrimp and get your finger. They don't take your finger off, but you do get little nips and bites. Nothing serious. Probably the stranding department has to worry more getting bitten by a seal they are trying to rescue who is sick."

Advice from Heather Urquhart

"Volunteer, volunteer, volunteer. That's the best bet. Not only will the people who work at the institution get to know your work, but you'll get an idea of what you'd be getting into, too.

"The glamourous part is that you get to work with a lot of cute baby animals. But the nonglamorous part is all that other stuff of being in a wet suit all day long and cold water, smelling like fish by the end of the day. Ninety percent of working with animals is cleaning up after them. It's not for everyone.

"But if it is for you, then volunteering is the way to go. The vast majority of the people working here formerly volunteered here. We do pull from within our ranks.

"Also, make sure you go to school, but don't specialize too much early on. For the type of job I have, you'd need to have a biology or zoology degree, one of these general topics. Then if you get to do some volunteer work, you can see more clearly what area to focus on. You might decide you want to work in a lab or in education."

Jenny Montague, Assistant Curator/Animal Trainer

Jenny Montague is assistant curator in the marine mammals department at the New England Aquarium. Her position is equivalent to the supervisor job title in the fishes department. She has been with the aquarium since 1988.

Jenny Montague's Background

"I started working at Marine World/Africa USA in Vallejo, California, a marine mammal zoo combination, as a landscaper while I was still in high school. It was an odd existence for a while. I was desperately trying to get into marine mammals, so I'd be at Marine World at five in the morning to do landscaping, then I had to go to school, and afterwards I'd come back and work until dark.

"I did some community college, but I got hired into the marine mammals department at Marine World right out of high school as an assistant trainer. That was 1981. I stayed there for eight years and left there as a senior trainer and show manager. I came to Boston right after that as supervisor of marine mammals. The woman who is curator here had worked briefly at Marine World on a research project, so we got to know each other. When the supervisor position opened, she called me, and I said 'yes' pretty quickly. I was ready for a change. As much as I liked Marine World, I felt I had probably gone as far as I could go in the hierarchy. I was interviewed over the phone, and our history together clinched the deal."

Jenny Montague's Responsibilities

"I am basically a trainer who has worked her way up through the ranks to an assistant curator position. I do more paperwork than I'd like to, but my basic job right now is to oversee the training and health of the animals. I supervise eight staff people. They range from assistant trainer to senior trainer.

"We work with the colony or resident marine mammals, which include Atlantic harbor seals, California sea lions, and California sea otters. We are responsible for the training, the care, and the presentation to the public of these mammals. We are located next door to the aquarium on the floating barge, what they call the Barge Discovery. It's an indoor show because of the weather we have in Boston. There are between four and seven shows daily, divided up amongst our staff. Sometimes three or four staff members are involved in the presentation if we're working with more than one animal. I personally do about eight or ten shows a week."

Jenny Montague's Role as Animal Trainer

"We're interested in portraying to the public what the animals' backgrounds are, what their natural histories are, and also some of the conservation issues that surround them. We do that in what we hope is a fun and educational way. When people can get close to live animals, it makes an incredible impression on them. All different levels of trainers participate, from the assistant trainers to assistant curator level. We get out there with the animals and talk to the audience about the different animal behaviors, explaining how they are able to do what they do. We do a little about the physiology and the biology of the animals and also about the training techniques we use. We'll do a demonstration of some of the medical behaviors we have, such as brushing the animal's teeth. They are all trained to sit or lie still and allow a stethoscope to be put on them. They are trained to lie still for x-rays. They open their mouths to let the veterinarians look down their throats. They'll sit still for an eye exam.

"The training is for the medical care of the animals, but it's also for mental stimulation. We find that, like anyone, if they are stimulated mentally and physically, they are much happier and healthier animals than if they are just left alone. We feel that training is a very important part of animal management in zoos and aquariums.

"During the presentations, we encourage audience members to participate. We ask them if they can give suggestions as to what we can do as individuals to keep the ocean a safer place for the animals. And anybody that has an interesting idea gets to come down and meet the sea lion. They get to pat him and get a kiss.

"When we are doing training, we keep records of all the advances they make and what new steps they've accomplished. Each individual animal has a primary trainer. I happen to be primary trainer right now for Ballou, a six-year-old, male California sea lion. There are usually two primary trainers for each animal so every day can be covered. We are basically responsible for getting regular weights on the animals, looking at their diets, making sure they are getting the proper amounts of food. All of the fish we feed them is sent out for analysis so we know exactly how many calories and how many grams of fat are in each kind of fish. We run that through a formula and calculate the right amount based on the animal's age and weight.

"The two primary trainers work as a team and are responsible for deciding what the animal is going to learn, who of the two will train it, and what methods we'll use.

"Each animal has its own personality. With some animals, you can work on a particular behavior with for half an hour and do several repeats, and then they make a step. We have one sea lion that if we repeat things over and over and lead him slowly through little steps, he'll never forget what you've taught him. Another one, Guthrie, gets bored very easily, and he starts to add in his own special flair. We spend more time retraining him than training him, to get rid of all his extraneous stuff. But he's a howl, one of the most fun sea lions to work with.

"How many hours you spend on something depends a lot on the animals and how much they are enjoying it and want to work with you. Tyler, a thirteen-year-old sea lion, isn't too crazy about having his teeth touched, so we'll only do that once or twice at a time. But he does like the other medical behaviors. He loves to lie around for x-rays, and he likes the vets to touch him, but you really have to go slow with his mouth.

"We also do show behaviors, high jumps and hitting a ball, for example. One we're working on now is a gallop, which shows the audience how quickly the sea lions can run on land. We work the sea lions in conjunction with our harbor seals sometimes and there is a major difference in speed between the two. The sea lions are much faster. The seals slug along on their bellies; they're not the most graceful creatures on land. A lot of this might seem circusy, but we are actually just trying to demonstrate the natural behavior of the animal. They are taught to do porpoising, for example, which is a natural behavior; what we teach them is to do it on command.

"We also train for research behaviors. Recently we started a hearing study, and we're at the beginning stages of teaching the animals to allow us to put headphones on them. At the same time they're being taught to respond to a sound cue. We also taught a sea lion to distinguish between the size of two objects and choose the larger one."

Animal Training Methods

"We use three different training methods. Operant conditioning is the one most widely used. You break a behavior into small steps and you lead the animal through the steps, providing reinforcement along the way.

"Another method is called innovative. Where operant conditioning is based on repetition, with innovative, we are asking the animals to create something new. After they have a solid operant conditioning understanding, we give them an arbitrary signal, which is crossing our arms across our chest. They have no idea what it means, but they might confuse it with a signal they do know and will offer a behavior. At the beginning we reward the old behavior, but then we'll only reward every new behavior. We use a variety of reinforcers—fish, or some of the animals like to be scratched and rubbed down.

"You spend a lot of time trying to find what the animals enjoy. Some like particular toys, others like things like ice cubes. So, for example, after the signal, they might give a salute. We'll reward it, and then, because they are familiar with operant conditioning, they figure that if they do it again, they'll be rewarded again. But the next time we don't reinforce the salute. You can get a curious look from them at that point. We'll give the signal again, and, if the salute doesn't work yet again, they'll start to offer something else, whether it's a look in another direction, or moving their whiskers forward in a curious questioning look. All of those little subtle movements are rewarded, and they start coming up with some pretty wild things. The purpose of this is to stimulate their creativity. It allows them to do things they like to do, and it keeps them thinking. It also gives the training staff some ideas. A lot of times they'll come up with things we wouldn't have thought of. Our sea lion Zack used to carry some rings around on his flippers and slap them at the same time. He would have all his flippers going and then he'd roll over. It was this amazing little dance that he did.

"The third method is called mimicry training. We ask the animals to focus on us and copy what we do. We got the idea for this because they already did mimic us to some extent. Some of the things they'll mimic is turning around in a circle or hopping up or opening a mouth or making a sound. It's really fun, and the benefit of that is it gives them a whole different focus. They have to watch our whole bodies completely, instead of just the usual hand gestures."

The Upsides and Downsides

"One of the nicest things about the job is that you never run out of ideas, and you're able to try them out. It's different every day. On the downside, the hours are inconsistent, and you can't rely on a nine-to-five day. Most of our staff works four ten-hour days. We are open seven days a week. Something always comes up, though, that prevents you from a regular schedule, but then, on the other hand, that might be a good thing."

Advice from Jenny Montague

"My advice would be to find any one of the schools that works with animal behavior. The interesting part of this job is that there are different academic subjects that can help you, such as psychology, animal behavior, and some zoology. Marine biology, however, is not a direct lead to the training field. It's a misconception a lot of people have. When I was in school it was pretty difficult finding people who were doing animal behavior work. It was happening, but it wasn't as accessible as it is today. It wasn't really considered a career path, and if you wanted to work with animal behavior, you did training with pigeons and rats. There are formal training schools now. One is EATM, Exotic Animal Training and Management, in Moorpark, California. (You will find the address in the Appendix.) There is also a strong program at the University of California in Santa Cruz. IMATA (International Marine Animal Trainers Association) can provide a list of all the training programs. (IMATA's address is also in the Appendix.)

"I also strongly suggest that people volunteer. A lot of times folks come and see animal shows, and they think that's all there is to it. But it isn't. We're up to our elbows in sinks full of dead fish all the time. We're running around in rubber boots all the time, and you do get damp. There's a lot more to it than the time on the stage. As a volunteer, you get a sense of all that.

"It is also important to visit different institutions. Everyone has a different style."

Becoming a Certified Diver

There are four or five nationally and internationally recognized certifying agencies. Future aquarists are responsible for obtaining this training and should do so in most instances before applying for an aquarist's position. Many university physical education departments offer diver training. It can also be pursued privately, through the YMCA or local dive shops. There full services are offered, including equipment use as well as training. A glance through the phone book will point you in the right direction. More information is provided in Chapter 8.

Help Finding That Job

Personnel Offices
A good source for job announcements is the personnel department of a specific government agency, private company, educational institution, or museum, zoo, marine park, or aquarium.

Publications
The Chronicle of Higher Education is a journal that lists academic positions at junior colleges, colleges, and universities. For

more information on obtaining academic positions, you can write to *The Chronicle* at 1255 Twenty-third Street NW, Washington, DC 20037.

The American Geophysical Union, whose address is below, publishes *Eos*, a weekly newspaper that lists employment opportunities, particularly in the government and with universities. Other technical journals carry similar postings.

Many manufacturing companies with significant interest in the oceans advertise in *Sea Technology*.

Other manufacturers, consulting firms, and universities to consider as potential employers are listed among the corporate sponsors of the Marine Technology Society, and their names are listed in each issue of the society's journal. For more information, write to

Marine Technology Society
1825 K Street NW, Suite 203
Washington, DC 20006

A book describing university curricula in oceanography and related fields may be obtained by writing to

Marine Technology Society
1828 L Street NW, Suite 906
Washington, DC 20036

The following organizations offer publications and information packets on a variety of aquatic science careers.

Earth Work Career Publications Service
SCA, Attn: Earth Work
P.O. Box 550
Charlestown, NH 03603
    (various publications on environmental careers)

Careers in Oceanography
American Geophysical Union
2000 Florida Avenue NW
Washington, DC 20009

Careers in Oceanography and Marine-Related Fields
The Oceanography Society
1755 Massachusetts Avenue NW, Suite 700
Washington, DC 20036

The Environmental Sourcebook
Lyons & Burford
31 West Twenty-first Street
New York, NY 10010

*Marine Education: A Bibliography of Educational Materials
    Available from the Nation's Sea Grant College Programs*
Sea Grant Marine Education Bibliography
Gulf Coast Research Laboratory
J. L. Scott Marine Education Center and Aquarium
P.O. Box 7000
Ocean Springs, MS 39564

*Marine Science Careers: A Sea Grant Guide to Ocean
    Opportunities*
Sea Grant Communications Office
University of New Hampshire
Kingman Farm
Durham, NH 03824

*Ocean Opportunities—a Guide to What the Oceans Have
    to Offer*
Marine Technology Society
2000 Florida Avenue NW, Suite 500
Washington, DC 20009

Opportunities in Marine and Maritime Careers, second
edition, by W. R. Heitzman with a foreword by Jean-Michel
Cousteau. Lincolnwood, Ill.: VGM Career Horizons, a
division of NTC/Contemporary Publishing Group.

*Peterson's Annual Guide to Undergraduate Study, Four Year
Colleges*
Department 6608, P.O. Box 2123
166 Bunn Drive
Princeton, NJ 08543

*Peterson's Guide to Graduate Programs in the Biological and
Agricultural Sciences*
Department 6608, P.O. Box 2123
166 Bunn Drive
Princeton, NJ 08543

Sea Technology Buyer's Guide
Annual Directory, Section F
Educational Institutions
Compass Publications, Inc.
1117 North Nineteenth Street, Suite 1000
Arlington, VA 22209

Training and Careers in Marine Science
International Oceanographic Foundation
3979 Rickenbacker Causeway
Miami, Florida 33149

U.S. Ocean Scientists & Engineers Directory
American Geophysical Union
2000 Florida Avenue NW
Washington, DC 20009

Networking

Although what you know is very important, who you know also helps. Many job openings are never officially announced, but are filled by personal recommendations. Volunteers or interns at an organization already have a foot well placed in the door.

A professor might recommend a graduate student he or she is supervising to a colleague. An informal interview at a scientific conference you attend could result in a job offer.

Internet

More and more organizations post information and job openings on the Web. Fire up any search engine and type in key words such as *biology careers* or *jobs with marine mammals*, and you'll be surprised at the number of resources you'll find.

Selected Internships

Internships are an excellent way to get your foot in the door. When an opening comes up, employers would rather hire someone they know and have worked with. They can also provide interns with referrals to other job opportunities and good recommendations to go along with future job applications.

Aquarium for Wildlife Conservation
610 Surf Avenue
Brooklyn, NY 11240

Aquarium of Niagara Falls
Intern/Volunteer Program
701 Whirlpool Street
Niagara Falls, NY 14301

Atlantic Cetacean Research Center
Intern/Volunteer Program
70 Thurston Point Road
P.O. Box 1413
Gloucester, MA 01930

Belle Isle Zoo & Aquarium
Intern/Volunteer Program
P.O. Box 39
Royal Oak, MI 48068

Center for Coastal Studies
Intern Review Committee
Box 1036
Provincetown, MA 02657

Center for Marine Conservation
Intern/Volunteer Program
1725 DeSales Street NW
Washington, DC 20036

Cetacean Research Unit
Intern/Volunteer Program
P.O. Box 159
Gloucester, MA 01930

Chicago Zoological Park
Brookfield Zoo
Intern/Volunteer Program
3300 Golf Road
Brookfield, IL 60513

Clearwater Marine Aquarium
249 Windward Passage
Clearwater, FL 33767

Dolphins Plus
P.O. Box 2728
Key Largo, FL 33037

Florida Department of Environmental Protection
Florida Marine Research Institute
Intern/Volunteer Program
100 Eighth Avenue SE
St. Petersburg, FL 33701

The John G. Shedd Aquarium
Internship Coordinator
1200 South Lake Shore Drive
Chicago, IL 60605

Kewalo Basin Marine Mammal Laboratory
Intern Coordinator
1129 Ala Moana Boulevard
Honolulu, HI 96814

Marine Mammal Research Group
EPCOT Center Trailer #251
Walt Disney World Company
P.O. Box 10,000
Lake Buena Vista, FL 32830

Marine Mammal Research Program
Intern/Volunteer Program
Texas A&M University at Galveston
Department of Fisheries and Wildlife
4700 Avenue U, Building 303
Galveston, TX 77551

Mirage Hotel
Intern/Volunteer Program
P.O. Box 7777
Las Vegas, NV 89177

Mote Marine Laboratory
Coordinator of Intern/Volunteer Services
1600 Thompson Parkway
Sarasota, FL 34236

Mystic Marinelife Aquarium
Intern/Volunteer Program
55 Coogan Boulevard
Mystic, CT 06355

National Aquarium in Baltimore
Pier 3
501 East Pratt Street
Baltimore, MD 21202

National Museum of Natural History
Intern Coordinator, Education Office
Room 212, MRC 158
Smithsonian Institution
Washington, DC 20560

Friends of the National Zoo
Research Traineeship Program
National Zoological Park
Washington, DC 20008

New England Aquarium
Intern/Volunteer Program
Central Wharf
Boston, MA 02110

The Oceania Project (humpback whale research)
P.O. Box 646
Byron Bay
248N New South Wales, Australia
E-mail: oceania@nor.com.au

Pacific Whale Foundation
Intern/Volunteer Program
Kealia Beach Plaza
101 North Kihei Road, Suite 21
Kihei, HI 96753

Pinniped Learning & Behavior Project
Internships, Long Marine Lab
University of California
100 Shaffer Road
Santa Cruz, CA 95060

Tethys Research Institute
Viale G.B. Gadio 2
I-20121 Milano, Italy

Theater of the Sea
Intern/Volunteer Program
P.O. Box 407
Islamorada, FL 33036

Waikiki Aquarium
Intern/Volunteer Program
2777 Kalakaua Avenue
Honolulu, HI 96815

Whale Museum
Volunteer Coordinator
62 First Street North
P.O. Box 945
Friday Harbor, WA 98250

Whale Research Group
230 Mount Scio Road
Memorial University of Newfoundland
St. John's, NF A1C 5S7
Canada

Field Programs

While some internships provide interns with a stipend as well as college credit, others charge fees to the interns for the experience they receive. An internship you pay for with the right organization can open as many doors as an internship that pays you.

Cetacean Behavior Lab Internships
Department of Psychology
San Diego State University
San Diego, CA 92182

Coastal Ecosystems Research Foundation
2648 Tennis Creek
Vancouver, BC V6T 2E1
Canada
E-mail: info@cerf.bc.ca

EarthWatch
680 Mount Auburn Street
P.O. Box 403
Watertown, MA 02272

Green Volunteers
1 Greenleaf Woods Drive, #302A
Portsmouth, NH 03810
E-mail: info@greenvol.com
(An international list of more than a hundred volunteer
    opportunities worldwide. Includes many marine mammal
    projects. Short- and long-term term opportunities available.
    Some projects require a financial contribution.)

Mingan Island Cetacean Study
285 Green Street
St. Lambert, QC J4P 1T3
Canada

Oceanic Society Expeditions
Fort Mason Center, Building E
San Francisco, CA 94123

School for Field Studies
16 Broadway Street
Beverly, MA 01915

University Research Expedition Programs
University of California
Berkeley, CA 94720-6586

CHAPTER THREE

The Navy and the Coast Guard

M aintaining a strong national defense encompasses such diverse activities as running a hospital, commanding a tank crew, programming computers, operating a nuclear reactor, and repairing a helicopter. The military's occupational diversity provides educational opportunities and work experience in literally hundreds of occupations.

Military personnel hold managerial and administrative jobs; professional, technical, and clerical jobs; construction jobs; electrical and electronics jobs; mechanical and repair jobs; and many others. The military provides training and work experience for people who serve a single enlistment of three to six years of active duty, those who embark on a career that lasts twenty years or more, and those who serve in the U.S. Army, Navy, Marine, Air Force, Coast Guard Reserves, and Army and Air National Guard.

There are more than 360 basic and advanced military occupational specialties for enlisted personnel and almost as many for officers. More than 75 percent of these occupational specialties have civilian counterparts. And three branches of the armed forces—the U.S. Navy, Coast Guard, and the Marines Corps— offer aquatic types the chance to be at sea.

Working Conditions

Military life is more regimented than civilian life, and one who enlists must be willing to accept the discipline. It is important to remember that signing an enlistment contract obligates you to serve for a specified period of time.

Dress and grooming requirements are stringent, and rigid formalities govern many aspects of daily life. For instance, officers and enlisted personnel do not socialize together, and commissioned officers are saluted and addressed as "sir" or "ma'am." These and other rules encourage respect for superiors whose commands must be obeyed immediately and without question.

The needs of the military always come first. As a result, hours and working conditions can vary substantially. However, most military personnel not deployed on a mission usually work eight hours a day, five days a week.

While off duty, military personnel usually do not wear their uniforms and are free to participate in family and recreational activities like most civilians. Some assignments, however, require night and weekend work or require people to be on call at all hours.

All may require substantial travel. Depending on the service, assignments may require long periods at sea, sometimes in cramped quarters or lengthy overseas assignments in countries offering few amenities. Some personnel serve tours in isolated parts of the world, where they are subject to extreme cold or heat and the possibility of hostilities breaking out at any time.

Others, such as sailors on carrier flight-deck duty, have jobs that are hazardous even in noncombat situations.

During wartime, many military personnel engage in combat and find themselves in life-or-death situations. They rely on countless hours of training to produce teamwork that is critical to the success or failure of an operation and to protecting the lives of the individuals in their unit. Rapidly advancing military technology has made warfare more precise and lethal, further increasing the need for teamwork.

Noncombatants may also face danger if their duties bring them close to a combat zone. Even in peacetime, most members of the combat arms branches of the military participate in hazardous training activities.

Ship and air crews travel extensively, while others in the military are stationed at bases throughout the country or overseas. Military personnel are usually transferred to a new duty station every few years.

Military personnel enjoy more job security than their civilian counterparts. Satisfactory job performance generally assures military personnel steady employment and earnings, and many of their requirements, such as meals, clothing, and living quarters, are provided for them.

Employment Figures

About 1.5 million individuals are on active duty in the armed forces. The breakdown is as follows:

483,000 in the Army

405,000 in the Navy

383,000 in the Air Force

172,000 in the Marine Corps

35,000 in the Coast Guard

Military personnel are stationed throughout the United States and in many countries around the world. California, Texas, North Carolina, and Virginia account for more than one in three military jobs.

About 249,000 are stationed outside the United States. More than 100,000 of these are stationed in Europe (mainly in Germany) and in the Western Pacific area.

The Qualifications You'll Need

General Enlistment Qualifications

As it has since 1973, the military expects to meet its personnel requirements through volunteers. Enlisted members must enter a legal agreement called an enlistment contract, which usually involves a commitment to eight years of service. Depending on the terms of the contract, two to six years are spent on active duty, the balance in the reserves. The enlistment contract obligates the service to provide the agreed-upon options—job, rating, pay, cash bonuses for enlistment in certain occupations, medical and other benefits, occupational training, and continuing education. In return, enlisted personnel must serve satisfactorily for the specified period of time.

Requirements for each service vary, but certain qualifications for enlistment are common to all branches. Enlistees must be between the ages of seventeen and thirty-five, must be a U.S. citizen or immigrant alien holding permanent resident status, must not have a felony record, and must possess a birth certificate. Applicants who are seventeen must have the consent of a parent or legal guardian before entering the service.

Applicants must pass both a written examination—the Armed Services Vocational Aptitude Battery—and meet certain minimum physical standards such as height, weight, vision, and overall health.

All branches prefer high school graduation or its equivalent and require it for certain enlistment options. Single parents are generally not eligible to enlist.

People thinking about enlisting in the military should learn as much as they can about military life before making a decision. This is especially important if you are thinking about making the military a career. Speaking to friends and relatives with military experience is a good idea. Determine what the military can offer you and what it will expect in return. Then talk to a recruiter, who can determine if you qualify for enlistment, explain the various enlistment options, and tell you which military occupational specialties currently have openings for trainees. But bear in mind that the recruiter's job is to recruit promising applicants into the military, so the information he or she gives you is likely to stress the positive aspects of military life.

Ask the recruiter to assess your chances of being accepted for training in the occupation or occupations of your choice or, better still, take the aptitude exam to see how well you score. The military uses the aptitude exam as a placement exam, and test scores largely determine an individual's chances of being accepted into a particular training program. Selection for a particular type of training depends on the needs of the service, general and technical aptitudes, and personal preference. Because all prospective recruits are required to take the exam, those who do so before committing themselves to enlist have the advantage of knowing in advance whether they stand a good chance of being accepted for training in a particular specialty. The recruiter can schedule you for the Armed Services Vocational Aptitude Battery without any obligation. Many high schools offer the exam as an easy way for students to explore the possibility of a military career, and the test also provides insight into career areas where the student has demonstrated aptitudes and interests.

The Enlistment Contract

If you decide to join the military, the next step is to pass the physical examination and then enter into the enlistment contract. This involves choosing, qualifying, and agreeing on a number of enlistment options such as length of active duty time, which may vary according to the enlistment option. (Most active duty programs have enlistment options ranging from three to six years, although there are some two-year programs.) The contract will also state the date of enlistment and other options such as bonuses and types of training to be received. If the service is unable to fulfill its part of the contract (such as providing a certain kind of training), the contract may become null and void.

All services offer a "delayed entry program" by which an enlistee can delay entry into active duty for up to one year. High school students can enlist during their senior year and enter a service after graduation. Others choose this program because the job training they desire is not currently available but will be within the coming year, or because they need time to arrange personal affairs.

Women are eligible to enter almost all military specialties. Although many women serve in medical and administrative support positions, women also work as mechanics, missile maintenance technicians, heavy equipment operators, fighter pilots, and intelligence officers. Only occupations involving a high probability of direct exposure to combat are excluded—for example, the artillery and infantry branches of the army.

People planning to apply the skills gained through military training to a civilian career should look into several things before selecting a military occupation. First, they should determine how good the prospects are for civilian employment in jobs related to the military specialties that interest them. Second, they should know the prerequisites for the related civilian jobs. Many occupations require a license, certification, or a minimum level of education. In such cases, it is important to determine whether military training is sufficient to enter the civilian equivalent or, if not, what additional training will be required.

Following enlistment, new members of the armed forces undergo recruit training. Better known as "basic" training, recruit training provides a six- to eleven-week introduction to military life with courses in health, first aid, and military skills and protocol. Days and nights are carefully structured and include rigorous physical exercises designed to improve strength and endurance.

Following basic training, most recruits take additional training at technical schools that prepare them for a particular military occupational specialty. The formal training period generally lasts from ten to twenty weeks, although training for certain more technical occupations—nuclear power plant operator, for example—may take as much as one year. Recruits who are not assigned to classroom instruction receive on-the-job training at the first duty assignment.

Many service people get college credit for the technical training they receive on duty, which, combined with off-duty courses, can lead to an associate's degree through community college programs such as the Community College of the Air Force.

In addition to on-duty training, military personnel may choose from a variety of educational programs. Most military installations have tuition assistance programs for people wishing to take courses during off-duty hours. These may be correspondence courses or degree programs offered by local colleges or universities. Tuition assistance pays up to 75 percent of college costs. Also available are courses designed to help service personnel earn high school equivalency diplomas. Each service branch provides opportunities for full-time study to a limited number of exceptional applicants. Military personnel accepted into these highly competitive programs receive full pay, allowances, tuition, and related fees. In return, they must agree to serve an additional amount of time in the service. Other very selective programs enable enlisted personnel to qualify as commissioned officers through additional military training.

Officer Training

Officer training in the armed forces is provided through the federal service academies (military, naval, air force, and coast guard), the Reserve Officers Training Corps (ROTC), Officer Candidate School (OCS) or Officer Training School (OTS), the National Guard (State Officer Candidate School programs), the Uniformed Services University of Health Sciences, and other programs. All are very selective and are good options for those wishing to make the military a career.

Federal service academies provide a four-year college program leading to a bachelor of science degree. The midshipman or cadet is provided free room and board, tuition, medical care, and a monthly allowance. Graduates receive regular or reserve commissions and have a five-year active duty obligation or longer if entering flight training.

To become a candidate for appointment as a cadet or midshipman in one of the service academies, most applicants obtain a nomination from an authorized source (usually a member of Congress). Candidates do not need to know a member of Congress personally to request a nomination. Nominees must have an academic record of the requisite quality, college aptitude test scores above an established minimum, and recommendations from teachers or school officials; they must also pass a medical examination. Appointments are made from the list of eligible nominees.

Appointments to the Coast Guard Academy are made strictly on a competitive basis. A nomination is not required.

ROTC programs train students in about 950 Army, 60 Navy and Marine Corps, and 550 Air Force units at participating colleges and universities. Trainees take two to five hours of military instruction a week in addition to regular college courses. After graduation, they may serve as officers on active duty for a stipulated period of time, at the convenience of the service. Some may serve their obligation in the reserves or guard. In the last two years of an ROTC program, students receive a monthly allowance while attending school and additional pay for summer training. ROTC scholarships for two, three, and four years are available on a competitive basis. All scholarships pay for tuition and have allowances for subsistence, textbooks, supplies, and other fees.

College graduates can earn a commission in the armed forces through OCS or OTS programs in the Army, Navy, Air Force, Marine Corps, Coast Guard, and National Guard. These officers must serve their obligation on active duty.

People with training in certain health professions may qualify for direct appointment as officers. In the case of health professions students, financial assistance and internship opportunities are available from the military in return for specified periods of military service. Prospective medical students can apply to the Uniformed Services University of Health Sciences, which offers free tuition in a program leading to an M.D. degree. In return, graduates must serve for seven years in either the military or the Public Health Service. Direct appointments also are available for those qualified to serve in other special duties, such as the judge advocate general (legal) or chaplain corps.

Flight training is available to commissioned officers in each branch of the armed forces. In addition, the Army has a direct enlistment option to become a warrant officer aviator.

Advancement Opportunities

Each service has different criteria for promoting personnel. Generally, the first few promotions for both enlisted and officer personnel come easily; subsequent promotions are much more competitive. Criteria for promotion may include time in service and grade, job performance, a fitness report (supervisor's recommendation), and written examinations. Those people who are passed over for promotion several times generally must leave the military.

Career Outlook

Opportunities should be good in all branches of the armed forces through the year 2006 because many qualified youth prefer civilian employment. About 190,000 enlisted personnel and 15,000 officers must be recruited each year to replace those who complete their commitment or retire. Educational requirements will continue to rise as military jobs become more technical and complex; high school graduates and applicants with a college background will be sought to fill the ranks of enlisted personnel.

America's strategic position is stronger than it has been in decades. Although there have been reductions in personnel due to the reduction in the threat from Eastern Europe and Russia, the number of active duty personnel is now expected to remain about constant through 2006.

The armed forces' goal is to maintain a sufficient force to fight and win two major regional conflicts occurring at the same time. However, political events could cause these plans to change.

Salaries, Allowances, and Benefits

Most enlisted personnel start as recruits at Grade E-1; however, those with special skills or above-average education start as high as Grade E-4.

Most warrant officers start at Grade W-1 or W-2, depending upon their occupational and academic qualifications and the branch of service.

Most commissioned officers start at Grade O-1; highly trained officers—for example, physicians, engineers, and scientists—start as high as Grade O-3 or O-4.

The following shows military basic pay for the Navy and Coast Guard by selected grade and rank for active duty personnel with fewer than two years service.

Grade/Rank	Basic Monthly Pay
O-6 Captain	$3,638.40
O-5 Commander	$2,910.30
O-4 Lieutenant Commander	$2,452.80
O-3 Lieutenant	$2,279.40
O-2 Lieutenant (JG)	$1,987.80
O-1 Ensign	$1,725.90

Warrant Officers

W-2 Chief Warrant Officer	$1,848.60
W-1 Warrant Officer	$1,540.20

Enlisted Personnel

E-6 Petty Officer 1st Class	$1,360.80
E-5 Petty Officer 2nd Class	$1,194.30
E-4 Petty Officer 3rd Class	$1,113.60
E-3 Seaman	$1,049.70
E-2 Seaman Apprentice	$1,010.10
E-1 Seaman Recruit	$900.90

Allowances

In addition to basic pay, military personnel receive free room and board (or a tax-free housing and subsistence allowance), medical and dental care, a military clothing allowance, military supermarket and department store shopping privileges, thirty days of paid vacation a year (referred to as leave), and travel opportunities.

Other allowances are paid for foreign duty, hazardous duty, submarine and flight duty, and employment as a medical officer.

Athletic and other recreational facilities such as libraries, gymnasiums, tennis courts, golf courses, bowling centers, and movies are available on many military installations.

Military personnel are eligible for retirement benefits after twenty years of service.

Veterans' Benefits

The Veterans Administration (VA) provides numerous benefits to those who have served at least two years in the armed forces. Veterans are eligible for free care in VA hospitals for all service-connected disabilities regardless of time served; those with other medical problems are eligible for free VA care if they are unable to pay the cost of hospitalization elsewhere. Admission to a VA medical center depends on the availability of beds, however. Veterans are also eligible for certain loans, including home loans. Regardless of health, a veteran can convert a military life insurance policy to an individual policy with any participating company in the veteran's state of residence. Job counseling, testing, and placement services are also available.

Veterans who participate in the New Montgomery GI Bill Program receive educational benefits. Under this program, armed forces personnel may elect to deduct from their pay up to $100 a month to put toward their future education for the first twelve months of active duty. Veterans who serve on active duty for three years or more, or two years active duty plus four years in the Selected Reserve or National Guard, will receive $427.87 a month in basic benefits for thirty-six months. Those who enlist and serve for less than three years will receive $347.65 a month. In addition, each service provides its own additional contributions to put toward future education. This sum becomes the service member's educational fund. Upon separation from active duty, the fund can be used to finance an education at any VA-approved institution.

Information on educational and other veterans' benefits is available from VA offices located throughout the country.

Close-Ups

With so many different career opportunities offered by the Navy and Coast Guard, it would be impossible to provide you with a representative sample of firsthand accounts in all the various fields. As mentioned earlier, you should make every effort to talk to people in the service to get a clear picture of whether this would be the life for you. What follows are accounts from two people in the Navy. They are currently doing similar work but took different paths to arrive there.

James Roman Stilipec,
U.S. Navy Journalist

Petty Officer Third Class James Roman Stilipec is a public affairs staff writer with the U.S. Navy, currently stationed aboard the USS *Carl Vinson*. He has been in the Navy since 1996. His home town is North Pole, Alaska.

James Stilipec's Background

"Before I joined the Navy, I never really saw the point of the military. I figured the world would be at peace in a few decades, and the military wasn't that necessary. I've wanted to be a creative writer since I was in eighth grade, and I have tons of ideas and stories I'm working on. In school, I never took journalism or worked with the yearbook because I felt it dealt too much with facts and not enough with fiction.

"Two years after high school I was selling women's shoes at the local JC Penney, and I was getting bored. I received a letter from the Navy asking if I would like information on any of the programs they offered. My father had been in the Navy for six years back in the seventies, and he spoke highly of it. I'd always had a passing interest in naval aviation and ships as well. So I indicated a few programs that sounded interesting and sent the letter off. Three months later I got a call from the Navy recruiter in Anchorage, Alaska, who persuaded me to fly to Anchorage for the weekend and take a military equivalence exam.

"I flew down, took the test, and scored very high. They then asked me what job I would like. I asked for something in communications, and eventually they turned up the position of journalist. I looked at a sheet that indicated a journalist's duties and realized they work alone or with little supervision, require good physical appearance and speaking skills, get to deal with people, and need a certain degree of creativity. I accepted the job and went on delayed entry, which meant I was technically in the Navy, but wouldn't go to boot camp for six months. The rest is history.

"The Navy provided me all my training at the Defense Information School (DINFOS) in Fort Meade, Maryland. I was flown there immediately following boot camp and began my training. The school teaches print and broadcast journalism, basic photography, and public affairs to all five military branches. I schooled with Marines, Army soldiers, Air Force airmen, and Coast Guard sailors along with my own Navy sailors.

"The school was divided into two parts: print journalism and public affairs, and TV and radio broadcasting. First, I learned the print side of journalism. This took three months and included public affairs training, basic photography, and a final project—a newspaper produced by the entire class.

"After this school I was a Navy journalist, but I still had the broadcasting side to learn. After a month in Norfolk, Virginia, working at the Fleet Home Town News Center, I returned to DINFOS for my broadcasting course. This class taught me basic announcing skills, electronic news gathering, radio broadcasting, and television studio skills. I graduated from this course on my twentieth birthday, February 22, 1995.

"My first assignment after DINFOS was the Naval Media Center Broadcast Detachment in Rota, Spain. I'd never been out of the United States, let alone overseas, in my life, so it was quite a nerve-wracking experience for me. When I arrived, I found my coworkers to be friendly and more than willing to help me out. One of them even went through the print journalism course with me, so it was nice to have a familiar face. In Spain I handled the cable TV programming that we provided for the base, shot and produced news stories for our five- to ten-minute newscasts, anchored the newscasts, produced TV and radio commercials, and produced two two-hour radio shows—a country show and a rock-and-roll show. All this hands-on training was incredibly helpful, allowing me to apply the theory I'd learned in school to my actual job."

The Next Step

"My tour in Spain was only to last two years, so within six months of my transfer, I had to look for orders to another location. After three months of searching, I found out there was an opening on board USS *Carl Vinson*, an aircraft carrier homeported in Bremerton, Washington. I jumped at the orders for a few reasons. One: I wanted to be closer to my home state of Alaska. In my two years in Spain, I'd only returned home once, and no relatives ever came to visit. Two: I'd wanted to get on a ship since I joined the Navy. I see ships as the 'real Navy,' and the chance to get stationed on one, and a carrier at that, was a dream come true. Three: I knew that on a carrier I would get a much more hands-on training in all the things I'd learned in school. In Spain I'd only exercised my broadcasting muscles. On a ship I would do print, radio, TV, public affairs, and much more."

What the Work Is Like

"Working at sea is much like working on the shore, except that you work and sleep and play in the same place. At first it's hard to get used to not being able to leave the ship, but soon you find other ways to entertain yourself in your time off. Reading, working out, and correspondence are popular pastimes. Also there are drills that the entire ship must participate in on a regular basis. One minute you're working on a story, the next you're fighting a fire in a smoke-filled space. Life on a carrier is unlike life anywhere else in the world. The ship is truly a floating city, with a post office, power plant, airport, sewer system, housing, lookout peak, cafeteria, 7-11, shopping mall, bank, cable TV, and radio stations.

"When we're in port or at sea, we have visitors that come onboard. It's up to my coworkers and me to see that these visitors get tours of the ship and are properly taken care of. We handle everything from film crews to generals, CEOs to elementary school classes.

"Also, while we are underway, we put out a daily four-page newspaper for the crew. I am required to write stories about things happening onboard the ship to keep the crew informed. The ship has more than 5,500 crewmembers, and everyone has a specific job and work environment. There are some areas of the ship that some sailors might never go to, so I try to let them know what the people who work in those other spaces are like. Aside from these duties, I also monitor all the training in my division, deal with ordering and purchasing new items for my division, maintain the equipment, produce a radio show, and keep our spaces clean.

"It can be hectic at times—when I have two long-term projects I'm working on, and my boss wants me to run something to the print shop and stop by the photo lab on the way back to get some pictures, and I need to get to an interview in twenty minutes and finish writing the story about the weapons department while trying to remember to order a new printer and toner cartridges for the copier. I've learned that it is possible to get everything done through proper time management and persistence. If you're in the middle of something and are sent on an errand, when you get back from that errand, return to what you were doing. Eventually everything will get done. And if you don't have anything to do, ask someone if you can help them out. Everyone else is just as busy as you are, and if you can help them out, then everyone gets the job done faster, and there's more time to relax at the end of the day."

A Typical Day at Sea
"In port I work a basic 7 A.M. to 4 P.M. day, Monday through Friday. At sea we work every day from 7 A.M. to anywhere from 6 P.M. to midnight.

"I wake up at 6 A.M., shower, shave, dress, and go to breakfast. I muster with my division a 7:15 A.M., and then we have a morning meeting during which my boss gives out daily duties. These vary from handling distinguished visitors to touch-up painting a wall.

"At 7:45 A.M. the whole ship conducts cleaning for an hour. At 8:45 A.M. I'm off to handle whatever duties my boss has given me. Sometimes I have an interview to conduct or paperwork to sort or a story to write. We also handle the shipboard television. We have a collection of eight hundred movies that we run on two shipboard channels to entertain the crew. We also run one channel with training tapes and general information for the crew.

"Around 11 A.M. I go down to eat lunch, set up an interview, and double-check the spelling of a sailor's name in personnel. I go on the radio at noon and do a two-hour rock-and-roll show. In the booth with me is another sailor who I am training to run the equipment so he can volunteer to do a show himself. After the show I set up the radio programming for the next day, figuring out when volunteers will be on the air, when my coworkers are doing a show, and when we will just be playing from our CD changers.

"At 4 P.M. I head to dinner and stop by the photo lab to pick up the pictures for the interview I did that morning. After dinner I start working on my story for the day and help a coworker to decide what movies will be played next week.

"Around 6 P.M. I have to take a camera crew up to the flight deck so they can get footage of our planes taking off and landing. At 8 P.M. I finish the story and E-mail it to the newspaper editor. While I'm on the computer, I write up a paragraph about the ship's activities for the day and send it to the website master to be posted on our Web page.

"Finally, at 9 P.M., my boss says I can head out, so I go down to my sleeping area (berthing) and pull out my laptop to work on a story idea I've been toying with for a week. I get into bed around 11 P.M. and read until I get drowsy and fall asleep."

The Upsides and Downsides

"There are many interesting sides to my job. I get to meet new people almost every day. I get to learn about all the parts of the ship and what everyone does. I get to meet the people who visit the ship and see their reactions to it. And I get to write stories about the Navy for newspapers all over the country.

"My work center is easy to work in for several reasons. First off, there aren't many of us. My whole division only has seven personnel in it, compared to other divisions that can have nearly a hundred. For the most part we all get along, and no one is left out of a division function. My boss and editor share a great sense of humor, and we get along very well. There are times that I come to heads with my coworkers, but they are rarely over work-related items and are usually differences of opinion.

"Because we're all journalists and know what it's like to deal with someone editing your story, we all tend to take criticism very well and are usually willing to listen to a new idea. Also, my coworkers usually come up with good ideas, and, when we implement them, everyone is happy because work is reduced and free time is increased. Many ideas deal with story writing or video production, and when the creativity is flowing, great ideas abound.

"For the most part, everyone knows when to get out of everyone else's way when they're busy, because they know what it's like to have a deadline. So I think we work well together because we know how to help and avoid each other at the right times.

"I like getting my stories put out to the public, producing an interesting radio show, being recognized for my achievements, and knowing that what I do influences people in one way or another—whether it's a sailor who learns something new about the ship she's on or it's a high school student who decides to join the Navy after a tour.

"Some boring aspects are the things we have to do on a daily or weekly basis, like cleaning and preventative maintenance. I know these things are important, but that doesn't make them exciting.

"I dislike the long hours, rude people, bad interviews, and people who think my job is the easiest thing in the world. Everyone in the Navy works hard in one way or another. I may not get greasy in my job, but what I do is important, it's time-consuming, and it requires plenty of knowledge as well as imagination.

"As an E-4 in the U.S. Navy, I make about $1,300 per month before taxes. Salary in the Navy is based on your rank, how long you've been in, and what benefits you're entitled to. Some benefits include sea pay, submarine pay, and a basic allowance for housing."

Advice from James Stilipec

"The Navy is a great place to start out your postlearning life. Much of the training is directly transferable to the civilian world. You should get to travel and see things you may have never seen in your life. But it is not for the fainthearted, and it is very different from civilian life. Honor, courage, and commitment are the core values of the Navy. If you join, realize in advance that it's not like camp."

David Butts, Deputy Public Affairs Officer

David Butts has been in the U.S. Navy since 1976. He is a senior chief journalist and is James Roman Stilipec's supervisor. He has earned 140 credits toward his B.A. with a double major in sociology and journalism/communications or history and will finish when he returns to shore duty. He has also attended various school and training programs offered by the Navy, such as firefighting, print and broadcast journalism, communications, and others. He is stationed aboard the USS Carl Vinson, and he is currently in the Persian Gulf.

David Butts' Background

"I was interested in the Navy first for the travel opportunities, second for the educational benefits. I chose the journalist career field because of my interest in writing, public speaking, and other communications areas.

"My first training was six months of courses in the basics of print and broadcast journalism at the Defense Information School. While there, I learned public relations theory, writing, photography, layout, and design—a lot of basic information crammed into long days of classroom work.

"Since then, I have returned to that school for intermediate photojournalism school and broadcast station manager's school.

"My first step in joining the Navy was seeing a recruiter. Over the years, I have renegotiated my assignments to include a photo-journalist job with *Stars and Stripes* in the Philippines, news director of the American Forces Network in Korea, a tour in the Persian Gulf, and a number of other challenging positions. I was editor of two Navywide publications. One, titled *LINK*, is a professional bulletin for all enlisted personnel in the Navy. The other, *All Hands*, is a monthly feature and news magazine about the Navy and its people. Both have print runs of nearly 100,000.

"For my current job, I had a discussion with my detailer, which is a Navy assignment counselor. He and I both felt this was a challenging job, offering many opportunities and rewards. So far, it has. The public affairs office of an aircraft carrier is the hub of a Navy battlegroup's public relations program—and the battle-group is often the first military force dispatched to any emergency or contingency worldwide. Since there are only twelve aircraft carriers in the Navy, there are only twelve people Navy-wide at a time who hold this type job. That is exciting in itself."

What the Work Is Like

"I have had the opportunity to work as a newspaper reporter and photojournalist in the Philippines, news director and executive producer in Korea, traveled to fifteen countries and some thirty states. Every two or three years, I transfer to a new job and a new place, sometimes working pretty standard forty-hour weeks, but many jobs require nearly twice that.

"Being on a ship is demanding but has many personal rewards. I like working with young men and women who bring fresh ideas and energy to the workplace. I like serving my country and at the same time doing what I love to do—work in public relations and journalism. This job offers the best of everything.

"I have five journalists working for me. Together, we publish a ship's daily newspaper, run twenty-four-hour-a-day radio and TV stations, handle media inquiries and information requests from the public, and produce special training videos.

"Each of us also has a second job onboard—we are in a repair locker damage-control team for general quarters, often called battle stations. In an emergency, we are also integrated into this team to fight fires, stop flooding, save lives—whatever is happening, we have to be prepared to handle it. So training for both our regular jobs and our general quarters jobs takes up a part of our day. I try to hit the gym at about 3 P.M. every day—that is about the midway point in my workday, and it gets me charged up for the rest of our work. We usually finish laying out and proofreading the newspaper at about 10 P.M. If I don't have any other urgent work, I usually go to bed at about 11 P.M. At sea, we work this schedule seven days a week. In port, we don't have to run the radio or TV station, and our newspaper is a weekly then, so we go home about 4 P.M. daily. In port we often give tours to the schools or media and arrange interviews with crew members."

The Upsides and Downsides

"My favorite part of my job is that it is always changing. I never get bored. My least favorite part is that it is always changing, so that it is hard to develop a routine.

"Actually, the biggest downside of Navy life is the separation from our families. We can write letters, send E-mail, even briefly talk on the phone while at sea, but there is no replacement for being there with them.

"This year my ship will be gone for Veterans Day, Thanksgiving, Christmas, New Year's, Martin Luther King Day, Presidents' Day, Valentine's Day, Easter, and my birthday. Six months straight. While there is no way to regain those missed special occasions, it helps knowing that we are doing something for our country. We are deployed at the holidays so others can enjoy them in peace, safe from danger.

"Exploring foreign ports is great fun, but it is something I'd rather share with my family. Being in the military in general has some pluses and minuses. I like the job security and benefits, while I think our pay lags behind some.

"Navy salaries start at about $900 a month, plus food and lodging. Benefits and pay increase with rank and length of service. My grade is E-8, and I make probably $40,000 annually, if you include some of the great benefits such as tuition assistance, medical, and dental."

Advice from David Butts

"Navy life requires discipline and a sense of personal responsibility. It gives young people an excellent opportunity to learn a skill, gain experience, and mature.

"The Navy will train you. You have to decide if you want to make a commitment, then if you are willing to give it your best. Talk to recruiters from different services, then weigh your options. Talk to your family and people you know who have been in the Navy. Talk to your guidance counselor at school. Decide what career you want to pursue, then see if the Navy offers a program in that area. Joining the Navy is not for everyone. It isn't always easy. One big difference between the Navy and many jobs is that after giving new sailors training, we also hand them responsibilities they could never imagine elsewhere. We have eighteen-year-old men and women steering this 95,000-ton ship.

I've seen eighteen-year-olds drive cars back home, and I wouldn't trust many of them with my life. But we teach them how; we stand by to catch them if they stumble; we give the full faith and confidence to do the job right; and we expect they will succeed. We are seldom disappointed.

"The men and women who join the Navy represent a cross section of America. But they also represent the best America has to offer. Back in their hometowns, these young men and women are heroes. Their moms and dads and grandparents and brothers and sisters are all very proud of what our sailors do. To me, being around all of these heroes makes mine the best job in the world."

CHAPTER FOUR

Commercial Fishing

F ishers gather aquatic species for human consumption, animal feed, bait, and other uses. Gathering fish hundreds of
miles from shore with commercial fishing vessels—large
boats capable of hauling a catch of tens of thousands of pounds
of fish—requires a crew that includes a captain, or skipper, a first
mate, and sometimes a second mate, boatswain, and deckhands.

Job Titles in Commercial Fishing

Captain

The captain plans and oversees the fishing operation—the fish
to be sought, the location of the best fishing grounds, the
method of capture, the duration of the trip, and the sale of the
catch.

The captain ensures that the fishing vessel is in suitable condition; oversees the purchase of supplies, gear, and equipment
such as fuel, netting, and cables; and hires qualified crew members and assigns their duties. The vessel's course is plotted with
navigation aids such as compasses, sextants, and charts; crew
members use electronic equipment such as autopilots, a loran system, and satellites to navigate.

The ships also use radar to avoid obstacles and depth sounders
to indicate the water depth and the existence of marine life
between the vessel and sea bottom. The captain directs the
fishing operation through the officers and records daily activities

in the ship's log. Upon returning to port, the captain arranges for the sale of the catch directly to buyers or through a fish auction and ensures that each crew member receives the prearranged portion of the adjusted net proceeds from the sale of the catch.

First Mate

The first mate—the captain's assistant, who must be familiar with navigation requirements and the operation of all electronic equipment—assumes control of the vessel when the captain is off duty. These duty shifts, called "watches," usually last six hours. The mate's regular duty, with the help of the boatswain and under the captain's oversight, is to direct the fishing operations and sailing responsibilities of the deckhands. These include the operation, maintenance, and repair of the vessel and the gathering, preservation, stowing, and unloading of the catch.

Boatswain or Deckhand

The boatswain, a highly experienced deckhand with supervisory responsibilities, directs the deckhands as they carry out the sailing and fishing operations. Prior to departure, the boatswain directs the deckhands to load equipment and supplies, either manually or with hoisting equipment, and untie lines from other boats and the dock. When necessary, boatswains repair the fishing gear, equipment, nets, and accessories. They operate the gear, letting out and pulling in nets and lines. They extract the catch, such as pollock, flounder, menhaden, and tuna, from the nets or lines' hooks. Deckhands use dip nets to prevent the escape of small fish and gaffs to facilitate the landing of large fish. The catch is then washed, salted, iced, and stowed away. Deckhands also must ensure that decks are clear and clean at all times and that the vessel's engines and equipment are kept in good working order. Upon return to port, they secure the vessel's lines to and from the docks and other vessels. Unless "lumpers," or laborers, are hired, the deckhands unload the catch.

Large fishing vessels that operate in deep water generally have more technologically advanced equipment, and some may have facilities on board where the fish are processed and prepared for sale. They are equipped for longer stays at sea and can perform the work of several smaller boats. (For information about merchant marine occupations, see Chapter 5.)

Some full-time and many part-time fishers work on small boats in relatively shallow waters and often in sight of land. Navigation and communication needs are modest, and there is little need for much electronic equipment or provisions for long stays at sea. Crews are small—usually only one or two people collaborate on all aspects of the fishing operation. This may include placing gill nets across the mouths of rivers or inlets, entrapment nets in bays and lakes, or pots and traps for shellfish such as lobsters and crabs. Dredges and scrapes are sometimes used to gather shellfish such as oysters and scallops.

A very small proportion of commercial fishing is conducted as diving operations. Depending upon the water's depth, divers—wearing regulation diving suits with an umbilical (air line) or a scuba outfit and equipment—use spears to catch fish and nets and other equipment to gather shellfish, coral, sea urchins, abalone, and sponges.

In very shallow waters, fish are caught from small boats having an outboard motor, from rowboats, or by wading. Fishers use a wide variety of hand-operated equipment—for example, nets, tongs, rakes, hoes, hooks, and shovels—to gather fish and shellfish, catch amphibians and reptiles such as frogs and turtles, and harvest marine vegetation such as Irish moss and kelp.

Sport Fishing

Although most fishers are involved with commercial fishing, some captains and deckhands are primarily employed in sport or recreational fishing. Typically a group of people charter a fishing vessel—for periods ranging from several hours to a number of days—for sport fishing, socializing, and relaxation and employ a captain and possibly several deckhands. (See the interview with charter skipper and sailing instructor, Lee Woods, in Chapter 8.)

Working Conditions

Fishing operations are conducted under various environmental conditions, depending on the waters and the kind of species being sought. Fishing vessels may be hampered or imperiled by storms, fog, or wind. Divers are affected by murky water and unexpected shifts in underwater currents.

Fishers can work under hazardous conditions, and often help is not readily available. Malfunctioning navigation or communication equipment may lead to collisions or even shipwrecks. Malfunctioning fishing gear poses the danger of injury to the crew, who also must guard against entanglement in fishing nets and gear, slippery decks resulting from fish processing operations, ice formation in the winter, or being swept overboard—a fearsome situation. Divers must guard against entanglement of air lines, malfunction of scuba equipment, decompression problems, or attacks by predatory fish. Treatment for serious injuries may have to await transfer to a hospital. And danger from incapacitating injuries is especially high. A disabled individual might die of injuries that could be routinely treated on land.

This occupation also entails strenuous outdoor work and long hours. Commercial fishing trips may require a stay of several weeks or even months hundreds of miles away from home port.

The pace of work varies—intense while netting and hauling the catch aboard and relatively relaxed while traveling between home port and the fishing grounds. However, lookout watches—usually six hours long—are a regular responsibility, and crew members must be prepared to stand watch at prearranged times of the day or night.

Although fishing gear has improved and operations have become more mechanized, netting and processing fish are strenuous activities. Even though newer vessels have improved living quarters and amenities such as television and shower stalls, crews still experience the aggravations of confined conditions, continuous close personal contact, and the absence of family.

Employment Figures

Fishers—along with hunters and trappers—hold an estimated 47,000 jobs nationwide. Approximately seven out of ten are self-employed. About half work part-time. Opportunities are best in the summer when demand for these workers peaks.

Captains, mates, and deckhands on fishing vessels account for the majority of jobs; hunters and trappers account for relatively few jobs.

Outside of the commercial fishing industry, some people employed in these occupations are involved in sport fishing activities. (For information on sport fishing, see Chapter 8.)

Employment of fishers is expected to decline through the year 2006. Fishing occupations depend on the natural ability of stock to replenish itself through growth and reproduction. Many operations are currently at or beyond maximum sustainable yield, and the number of workers who can earn an adequate income from fishing is expected to decline. Most job openings will arise from the need to replace workers who retire or leave the occupation.

Some fishers leave the occupation because of the strenuous and hazardous nature of the job and the lack of steady, year-round income. In many areas, particularly the North Atlantic, pollution and excessive fishing have adversely affected the stock of fish and, consequently, the demand for fishers. In some areas, states have greatly reduced permits to fishers, allowing stocks of fish and shellfish to replenish themselves, leaving many fishers without work.

Other factors contributing to the projected decline in employment of fishers include the use of more sophisticated electronic equipment for navigation, communication, and fish location; improvements in fishing gear, which have greatly increased the efficiency of fishing operations; and the use of highly automated "floating processors," where the catch is processed aboard the vessel.

Sport fishing boats will continue to provide some job opportunities for those interested.

The Qualifications You'll Need

Fishers generally acquire their occupational skills on the job, many as members of families involved in fishing activities. No formal academic requirements exist.

Under a Coast Guard legislative proposal, operators of federally documented commercial fishing vessels will be required to complete a Coast Guard–approved training course. Young people can expedite entrance into these occupations by enrolling in two-year vocational-technical programs offered by secondary schools, primarily in coastal areas.

In addition, the University of Rhode Island offers a bachelor's degree program in fishery technology that includes courses in seamanship, vessel operations, marine safety, navigation, vessel repair and maintenance, health emergencies, and fishing gear technology and is accompanied by hands-on experience.

Experienced fishers may find short-term workshops offered through various postsecondary institutions especially useful. These programs provide a good working knowledge of electronic equipment used in navigation and communication and the latest improvements in fishing gear.

Captains and mates on larger fishing vessels of at least two hundred gross tons must be licensed. Captains of sport fishing boats used for charter, regardless of size, also must be licensed. Crew members on certain fish-processing vessels may need a merchant mariner's document. These documents and licenses are issued by the U.S. Coast Guard to individuals who meet the stipulated health, physical, and academic requirements.

Fishers must be in good health and possess physical strength. Coordination and mechanical aptitude are necessary to operate, maintain, and repair equipment and fishing gear. They need perseverance to work long hours on the sea, often under difficult conditions.

On larger vessels, they must be able to work as members of a team. They must be patient yet alert to overcome the boredom of long watches when not engaged in fishing operations. The ability to assume any deckhand's functions on short notice is important. Mates must have supervisory ability and be able to assume any deckhand's and the captain's duties when necessary. The captain must be highly experienced, mature, decisive, and possess the necessary business skills. Captains with initiative and the required capital often become boat owners.

On fishing vessels, most fishers begin as deckhands. Deckhands whose experience and interests are in ship engineering—maintenance and repair of ship engines and equipment—can eventually become licensed chief engineers on large commercial vessels after meeting the U.S. Coast Guard's experience, physical, and academic requirements.

Divers in fishing operations can enter commercial diving activity—for example, ship repair and pier and marina maintenance—usually after completion of a certified training program sponsored by an educational institution or industry association. Experienced, reliable deckhands who display supervisory qualities may become boatswains. Boatswains may, in turn, become second mates, first mates, and finally captains.

Almost all captains become self-employed, and the overwhelming majority eventually own or have an interest in one or more fishing ships. Some may choose to run a recreational or sport fishing operation. When their seagoing days are over, experienced individuals may work in or, with the necessary capital, own stores selling fishing and marine equipment and supplies. Some captains may assume advisory or administrative positions in industry trade associations or government offices such as harbor development commissions or teaching positions in industry-sponsored workshops or in educational institutions.

Earnings

Median earnings of full-time fishers were about $390 a week in 1996, the latest figures available. The middle 50 percent earned between $280 and $480 a week. The highest-paid 10 percent earned more than $520, while the lowest-paid 10 percent earned less than $230.

Earnings of fishers generally are highest in the summer and fall—when demand for their services peaks and environmental conditions are favorable—and lowest during the winter. Many full-time and most part-time workers supplement their incomes by working in other activities during the off-season. For example, fishers may work in seafood processing plants, establishments selling fishing and marine equipment, or in construction.

Earnings of fishers vary widely depending upon the specific occupational function, the size of the ship, and the amount and value of the catch. The costs of the fishing operation—operating the ship, repair and maintenance of gear and equipment, and the crew's supplies—are deducted from the sale of the catch. The net proceeds are distributed among the crew members in accordance with a prearranged percentage.

Generally, the ship's owner—usually its captain—receives half of the net proceeds, which covers any profit as well as the depreciation, maintenance, and replacement costs of the ship.

CHAPTER FIVE

Water Transportation Careers

An Overview

Workers in water transportation occupations operate and maintain deep sea merchant ships, tugboats, towboats, ferries, dredges, research vessels, and other waterborne craft on the oceans and the Great Lakes, in harbors, on rivers and canals, and on other waterways.

Captains or masters are in overall command of the operation of a vessel, and they supervise the work of the other officers and the crew. They set course and speed, maneuver the vessel to avoid hazards and other ships, and periodically determine position using navigation aids, celestial observations, and charts. They direct crew members who steer the vessel, operate engines, signal to other vessels, perform maintenance, and handle lines (operate towing or dredging gear). Captains ensure that proper procedures and safety practices are followed, check that machinery and equipment are in good working order, and oversee the loading and unloading of cargo or passengers. They also maintain logs and other records of the ships' movements and of the cargo carried.

Captains on large vessels are assisted by deck officers or mates. Merchant marine vessels—those carrying cargo overseas—have a chief or first mate, a second mate, and a third mate. Mates oversee the operation of the vessel, or "stand watch" for specified periods, usually four hours on and eight off. On smaller vessels, there may be only one mate (called a pilot on some inland vessels) who alternates watches with the captain.

Engineers or marine engineers operate, maintain, and repair propulsion engines, boilers, generators, pumps, and other machinery. Merchant marine vessels usually have four engineering officers: a chief engineer and a first, second, and third assistant engineer. Assistant engineers each stand periodic watches, overseeing the operation of engines and machinery.

Deckhands, particularly on inland waters, operate the vessel and its deck equipment under the direction of the ship's officers and keep the nonengineering areas in good condition. They stand watch, looking out for other vessels, obstructions in the ship's path, and aids to navigation. They also steer the ship, measure water depth in shallow water, and maintain and operate deck equipment such as lifeboats, anchors, and cargo-handling gear. When docking or departing, they handle lines. They also perform maintenance chores such as repairing lines, chipping rust, and painting and cleaning decks and other areas. Deckhands may also load and unload cargo. On vessels handling liquid cargo, they hook up hoses, operate pumps, and clean tanks. Deckhands on tugboats or tow vessels tie barges together into tow units, inspect them periodically, and disconnect them when the destination is reached. Larger vessels have a boatswain or head deckhand.

Marine oilers work below decks under the direction of the ship's engineers. They lubricate gears, shafts, bearings, and other moving parts of engines and motors, read pressure and temperature gauges and record data, and may repair and adjust machinery.

A typical deep-sea merchant ship has a captain, three deck officers or mates, a chief engineer and three assistant engineers, plus six or more deckhands and oilers. Depending on their size, vessels operating in harbors, rivers, or along the coast may have a crew comprising only of a captain and one deckhand or as many as a captain, a mate or pilot, an engineer, and seven or eight deckhands. Large vessels also have a full-time cook and helper, while on small ones, a deckhand does the cooking. Merchant ships also have an electrician, machinery mechanics, and a radio officer.

Pilots guide ships in and out of harbors, through straits, and on rivers and other confined waterways where a familiarity with local water depths, winds, tides, currents, and hazards such as reefs and shoals is of prime importance. Pilots on river and canal vessels usually are regular crew members, like mates. Harbor pilots are generally independent contractors who accompany vessels while they enter or leave port. They may pilot many ships in a single day.

Merchant mariners are away from home for extended periods but earn long leaves. Most are hired for one voyage, with no job security after that. At sea, they usually stand watch for four hours and are off for eight hours, seven days a week. Those employed on Great Lakes ships work sixty days and have thirty days off but do not work in the winter when the lakes are frozen over. Workers on rivers and canals and in harbors are more likely to have year-round work. Some work eight- or twelve-hour shifts and go home every day. Others work steadily for a week or month and then have an extended period off. When working, they are usually on duty for six or twelve hours and are off for six or twelve hours.

People in water transportation occupations work in all kinds of weather conditions, and, although merchant mariners try to avoid severe storms while at sea, working in damp and cold conditions is unpleasant. It is uncommon for vessels to sink, but workers nevertheless face the possibility that they may have to abandon their craft on short notice if it collides with other vessels or runs aground. They also risk injury or death from falling overboard and hazards associated with working with machinery, heavy loads, and dangerous cargo.

Some newer vessels are air-conditioned, soundproofed from noisy machinery, and have comfortable living quarters.

Nevertheless, some workers do not like the long periods away from home and the confinement aboard ship.

The Training You'll Need

Entry, training, and educational requirements for most water transportation occupations are established and regulated by the U.S. Coast Guard. All officers and operators of watercraft must be licensed by the U.S. Coast Guard, which offers nearly sixty different licenses, depending on the position and type of craft. Licensing differs somewhat between the merchant marine and others.

Deck and engineering officers in the merchant marine must be licensed. To qualify for a license, applicants must have graduated from the U.S. Merchant Marine Academy or one of the six state academies and pass a written examination. A physical examination and a drug test are also required. People with at least three years of appropriate sea experience also can be licensed if they pass the written exam, but it is difficult to pass without substantial formal schooling or independent study. Also, because sailors may work six months a year or less, it can take five to eight years to accumulate the necessary experience.

The academies offer four-year bachelor's degree programs (one offers a three-year associate program) in nautical science or marine engineering to prepare students to be third mates or third assistant engineers. With experience and passing of additional exams, third officers may qualify for higher rank. Because of keen competition, however, officers may have to take jobs below the grade for which they are qualified.

For employment in the merchant marine as an unlicensed sailor, a merchant mariner's document is needed. Applicants for merchant marine documents do not need to be U.S. citizens. A medical certificate of excellent health and a certificate attesting to vision, color perception, and general physical condition may be required for higher-level deckhands. While no experience or formal schooling is required, training at a union-operated school is helpful. Beginners are classified as ordinary deckhands and may be assigned to the deck or engineering department. With experience at sea, and perhaps union-sponsored training, an ordinary deckhand can pass the able seaman exam.

Merchant marine officers and deckhands, both experienced and beginners, are hired for voyages through union hiring halls or directly by shipping companies.

Harbor pilot training is usually an apprenticeship with a shipping company or a pilot employees' association. Entrants may be able seamen or licensed officers.

No training or experience is needed to become a seaman or deckhand on vessels operating in harbors or on rivers or other waterways. Newly hired workers generally learn skills on the job. With experience, they are eligible to take a Coast Guard exam to qualify as a mate, pilot, or captain. Substantial knowledge gained through experience, courses in seamanship schools, and independent study are needed to pass the exam.

Career Outlook

Water transportation workers hold about 51,000 jobs nationwide. The following tabulation shows employment in the job titles that make up this group:

Ship captains and mates	21,000
Sailors and deckhands	22,000
Marine engineers	9,000

More than 1,400 of all the captains and pilots were self-employed, operating their own vessels, or were pilots who were independent contractors.

About 40 percent of all water transportation workers were employed onboard merchant marine ships or U.S. Navy Military Sealift ships operating on the oceans or Great Lakes. Another 40 percent were employed in transportation services, working on tugs, towboats, ferries, dredges, and other watercraft in harbors, on rivers and canals, and other waterways.

Others worked in water transportation services such as piloting vessels in and out of harbors, operating lighters and chartered boats, and in marine construction, salvaging, and surveying. The remaining water transportation workers were employed on vessels carrying passengers, such as cruise ships, casino boats, sightseeing and excursion boats, and ferries.

Keen competition is expected to continue for jobs in water transportation occupations. Overall, employment in water transportation occupations is projected to decline through the year 2006. Opportunities will vary by sector.

Employment in deep-sea shipping is expected to continue its long-term sharp decline as U.S.-staffed ships carry an even smaller proportion of international cargo. Stringent federal regulations require larger crews on U.S.-flagged ships, which allow vessels that fly foreign flags and have smaller crew sizes, to operate at lower cost and make a larger profit. A fleet of deep-sea U.S.-flagged ships is considered to be vital to the nation's defense, so some receive federal support through a maritime security subsidy, and other provisions in laws limit certain federal cargoes to ships that fly the U.S. flag.

Today's newer ships are designed to be operated safely by much smaller crews. Innovations include automated controls and computerized monitoring systems in navigation, engine control, watchkeeping, ship management, and cargo handling. As older vessels are replaced, crew responsibilities will change. Sailors will need to learn new skills to be able to handle these varied duties.

Vessels on rivers and canals and on the Great Lakes carry mostly bulk products such as coal, iron ore, petroleum, sand and gravel, grain, and chemicals. Shipments of these products are expected to grow through the year 2006, but productivity increases should cause employment to decline. Employment in water transportation services is likely to show little or no change.

The decline in new opportunities has created competition for existing jobs, with many experienced merchant mariners going for long periods without work. As a result, unions generally accept few new members. Also, many merchant marine academy graduates have not found licensed shipboard jobs in the U.S. Merchant Marine, although most do find industry-related jobs. Most are commissioned as ensigns in the U.S. Naval Reserve, and some may be selected for active duty in the Navy. Some find jobs as sailors on U.S.-flagged or foreign-flagged vessels, tug-boats, other watercraft, or civilian jobs with the U.S. Navy. Some take land-based jobs with shipping companies, marine insurance companies, manufacturers of boilers or related machinery, or other related jobs. Unless the number of people seeking mer-chant marine jobs declines sharply, the present intense compe-tition is likely to continue.

Earnings

Water transportation workers who usually worked full-time had median weekly earnings of $579 in 1996, the latest figures avail-able. The middle 50 percent earned between $402 and $860 a week. The lowest 10 percent earned less than $287, while the highest 10 percent earned more than $1,157 a week.

Captains and mates had median weekly earnings of $653 a week in 1996. The middle 50 percent earned between $394 and $904 a week. The lowest-paid 10 percent earned less than $275, while the highest 10 percent earned more than $1,203 a week.

Deckhands had median weekly earnings of $520 a week in 1996. The middle 50 percent earned between $395 and $695 a week. The lowest 10 percent earned less than $288 a week, while the highest 10 percent earned more than $983 a week.

Close-Up

Thomas MacPherson, Chief Engineer

Thomas MacPherson has had fourteen years sea time in the U.S. Navy and one year with Edison Chouest Offshore, an offshore support enterprise in Galiano, Louisiana.

Thomas MacPherson's Background

"I was in the Navy for eighteen years and retired early, just over a year ago. I chose joining the Navy to leave the area I grew up in (Mckeesport, Pennsylvania) because the steel industry was dying out and I wanted to see something different. My father and older brother were in the Navy as well.

"The job I am doing now is similar to what I knew in the Navy, although less intense and more informal—a lot more fun."

What the Work Is Like

"The type of boat I work on is an elevator support ship. My company's primary role is support of the oil industry by transporting crews and supplies to and from the oil rigs. We also transport what is called liquid mud—for pumping into the oil wells to displace the oil.

"My present position is chief engineer, and my duties are to supervise and operate the engine room and various engineering aspects of the boat. Log keeping, engine operation, fuel, water, electricity, and some electronics are required to be operated or maintained. For example, today I operated the diesel engines, worked on the phone lines, helped with the deckhands in a small boat, and operated the hydraulic system to lower the submarine elevator system.

"My company does a lot of work with various Navy projects, such as submarine testing and even the recovery of the USS *Monitor* propeller and shaft from off the coast of North Carolina.

"The most enjoyable part of the job is the maintenance and operation of the boats. I like to learn something new every day, and it's nice to get to work on something different from time to time. As long as it is done safely and correctly, there are very few things you can't do.

"The downside is the time that is spent away from home, but I actually enjoy going out to sea, getting away for a time to catch up on reading or movies. The pay is good, and it does provide food and a bunk. The pay is based on a day rate. Starting out as an oiler, $85 to $120 is normal. An assistant engineer can make from $150 to $200 a day, while a chief engineer earns $200 or more a day. It depends on your license, the company, the work location, and the boat contract."

Advice from Thomas MacPherson

"The qualities you should have include dependability, responsibility, patience, and, most importantly, you shouldn't be afraid of hard work.

"It is possible to shorten some requirements by attending one of the merchant marine academies, but for my case the U.S. Navy provided me with the prerequisites for my present license. Coast Guard or Navy sea time is partially credited toward merchant marine sea time.

"For the offshore vessel work I am in, knowledge of diesels is a prerequisite. For ocean vessels, steam and/or diesel knowledge is necessary. In both cases, electrical and fluid system knowledge are required.

"As for starting out, sea time is sea time. Whether going to the Gulf of Mexico (Louisiana and Texas), or Alaska, or even to the Northeast (Massachusetts or Rhode Island for the fishing fleet), all require some seagoing experience to get into the job.

"A lot of junior engineers start out as ordinary seamen (OS), or you can start out in the seagoing services (Navy or Coast Guard) as I did."

CHAPTER SIX

Cruise Staff

P robably everyone, at one time or another, has seen reruns of "The Love Boat" on television and watched Julie, Doc, Isaac, Gopher, and Captain Steubing go about their daily activities, interacting with passengers while ensuring that they have the best vacations of their lives.

Although the reality might not exactly mirror life on the popular series, being part of a cruise ship staff does let you make new friends and lead a carefree lifestyle.

The Different Jobs Aboard Ship

Cruise lines employ all sorts of personnel to handle the many tasks involved with running a ship. A smaller ship with 850 passengers might have more than 400 crew members; larger ships with 2,500 or so passengers employ up to 1,000 crew members.

The "marine crew"—the captain, deckhands, deck officers, oilers, engineering officers—generally come from the ship's point of origin—Greece, Norway, or Italy, for example—so most of the jobs open to Americans are found with the "hotel crew."

"Hotel Crew"

To fully understand what a cruise is like, think of it as a large hotel that floats. Just as hotels have different personalities and amenities, so do cruises. Some cruises are extremely luxurious, offering the best food and service, similar to staying at an elegant hotel. Other cruises are more casual and fun, filled with activities that cater to a younger crowd.

Whatever style the cruise, most employ crews to work in the following positions:

Accountant

Assistant Cruise Director

Beautician

Casino Operator

Cruise Director

Cruise Staff/Activities

Disc Jockey

Doctor/Nurse

Entertainer

Gift Shop Manager/Assistant

Port Lecturer

Photographer

Purser

Reservationist

Sales Manager

Shore Excursions Director

Sports/Fitness Director

Steward

Waiter

Youth Counselor

Job titles and responsibilities vary from ship to ship. For example, the term *cruise staff* is often synonymous with assistant cruise director or social or activities director.

What the Work Is Like

Although filled with its share of excitement and glamour, working on a ship involves a lot of hard work. Cruise staff put in long hours—anywhere from eight to fifteen hours a day, seven days a week—and must maintain a high level of energy and always be cordial and friendly to passengers.

Cruise staff members are generally involved with organizing activities and social events, including common shipboard games such as shuffleboard and ringtoss, bingo, aerobics classes, basketball, golf putting (and driving—off the stern of the ship), and pool games. They also participate in cocktail parties and masquerade balls and take every opportunity to make sure passengers feel comfortable and are enjoying themselves.

Many of the cruise staff also double as entertainers and need to have some talent for performing, whether as singers, musicians, or DJs.

When in port, most of the crew are allowed to go ashore and have time off to explore, although some cruise staff function as chaperones, helping passengers find their way around foreign locales.

Activities onboard ship usually follow a rigid schedule with little time in between for the crew to rest and take a break. With a constant eye on their watches, cruise staff run from one activity to another, announcing games over the loudspeaker, setting up the deck for exercise classes, supervising ringtoss tournaments or other special events, and encouraging everyone to participate.

An outgoing, energetic individual would be in his or her element in such a job; someone who lacks those skills would find the work very difficult.

Earnings

While salaries are not overly generous, the additional benefits are. Cruise staff are provided with free housing while onboard ship and all they can eat. It's not necessary for a full-time employee of a cruise line to maintain quarters ashore, and, therefore, most of the salary can be saved.

Cruise ships also sail to exotic ports, giving staff members the chance to travel and meet people from all over the world.

Assistant cruise directors and other cruise staff can move up the ladder to more supervisory and managerial positions. They need to demonstrate that they have organizational skills, that they can delegate and manage people. They also have to be good at detail work and paperwork.

Sometimes earning a promotion has to do with how much experience you have and how good you are—or perhaps with who has quit or died.

The Training You'll Need

A college education is not necessary, but some cruise lines prefer to see an applicant with a degree in psychology, hotel management, physical education, or communications. It's also a good idea to know another language, especially Spanish or German.

Even more important are the personal qualities a good cruise staff should possess:

Patience

Diplomacy

Tolerance for a wide variety of people

A never-ending supply of energy

An outgoing and genuinely friendly nature

Enthusiasm

Artistic talent

Athletic ability

Most successful applicants land their jobs by applying directly to the various cruise lines, which are located mainly in Miami and Fort Lauderdale, Los Angeles, San Francisco, and New York. Look through the Yellow Pages in each city for cruise line addresses and phone numbers or consult *How to Get a Job with a Cruise Line*, mentioned at the end of this chapter.

Close-Ups

Richard Turnwald, Cruise Ship Purser

Richard Turnwald has been working in the cruise industry for more than fourteen years. He started out shoreside, in the operations department, where he handled everything from personnel to ordering supplies for the ships. He went from there to positions with the cruise staff as a shore excursions director, assistant cruise director, and port lecturer providing information on the different ports of call. He then worked his way up the ranks from junior purser to chief purser.

Richard Turnwald's Background

"Ever since I was a little boy I've always loved ships and the sea. I read about them and studied them, and there was no doubt in my mind that I wanted to be involved in some way with ships as a profession.

"I was in college in Michigan studying travel and tourism, and I wanted to get involved with the cruise lines. I sent out my resume and wrote to the various cruise lines, most of which were based in Miami. I was interviewed over the telephone and was offered a position in the office. It was exciting and scary at the same time. I was just out of college, and I had to relocate to a place where I didn't know anyone, but it was like a dream for me to finally be able to work closely with the cruise ships."

What the Work Is Like

"The purser's office is like the front desk at a big hotel. The staff members handle all the money on the ship, pay all the bills and the salaries, cash traveler's checks for passengers, provide safes for valuables, fill out all the documentation for customs and immigration officials in the different countries, and perform all the other crucial behind-the-scenes functions.

"The purser is who passengers come to for information or help with problems. Pursers are in charge of cabin assignments, and they also coordinate with the medical personnel to help handle any emergencies.

"There are various ranks for a purser: junior or assistant purser, second purser, first purser, then chief purser. As chief purser I had a staff of six people I was responsible for; on larger ships the purser's office might have fourteen or fifteen people.

"Promotions are based on your ability—how well you do your job—as well as the length of time you've been employed. I was fortunate; I rose up through the ranks fairly quickly. Within three months I had worked my way up from junior purser to chief purser. But that's really an exceptional situation. It usually takes a good year or so. It depends on how many people are ahead of you, if they leave or stay.

"It can be competitive. You have to consider that there's only one chief purser on each ship. Some people start working on a ship and their only background was watching 'The Love Boat' and thinking from that how wonderful it would be. They don't have a realistic viewpoint of the downsides of cruise work.

"When you live and work on a ship, you're an employee, you're not there to be a passenger. The living conditions are not as luxurious as for the passengers; you might be sharing a room with one or two other crew members, and there's not a lot of privacy. There's a sense of confinement on a ship; you can't just go out to dinner whenever you want. Experiencing cabin fever is common. You live your job twenty-four hours a day, and there's no getting away from that.

"The food isn't as high class; passengers might be having lobster and steak upstairs; the crew is eating fish or meat loaf below. You might be away from home for the first time and feeling homesick and cut off. When you work on a ship, you're on duty seven days a week; you don't have a day off for several months at a time. Some people can get burned out on that, while others can thrive.

"If you take a positive approach, you realize that you don't have to commute to work or worry about housing. Though you don't get an entire day off, you get several hours at a time when you're in port, and you get to see a lot of wonderful things. I've been all over the world, to places I wouldn't have had the time or money to get to otherwise. I've been to the Caribbean, Alaska, South America, Antarctica, Europe, Hawaii. If you're on an itinerary that repeats every week, you get to know that place very well and the people there, so that's a plus.

"And there's something so relaxing and peaceful about being at sea, just to stand by the railing of the deck and see the changes in the weather and the whales and the other sea life. Another advantage is the money. You work hard and very intensely for long periods of time, but typically you're paid very well and it's a good opportunity to save money. I was able to buy a house."

Advice from Richard Turnwald

"Work on people skills, being friendly, being helpful and courteous. It's very important—you'll be representing the cruise line to a lot of people. And you have to be willing and able to accept orders. It isn't as strict as the Navy, but when you're on a ship there are a lot of rules and guidelines you have to follow. You've heard the expression, 'to run a tight ship'—you have to have regulations to do that. If you're too independent-minded and don't like to be told what to do, then ship life wouldn't be for you."

Beverley Citron, Assistant Cruise Director

Beverley Citron began working on cruise ships at the age of twenty-one as a hairdresser. Realizing she would enjoy being part of the social staff more, she took time off to gain the necessary skills. Her hard work paid off, and she landed her first job as a youth counselor. She also worked as a sports director, then was promoted to assistant cruise director.

Beverley Citron's Background

"I've wanted to work on a ship since I was five years old. I was influenced by two of my uncles who were in the English Royal Navy. Every time they came ashore they'd show me home movies they'd taken of the blue waters of Australia or Hong Kong. All through my school years it was my goal.

"I started out working as a social director for a holiday resort and my local sailing club in England looking after children, planning and implementing their activities. I studied singing and the guitar, then put together an act with musical arrangements and costumes. I was determined to get a job as a social staff member.

"After all those years of applying, when I got that letter in the mail saying 'Beverley, we have selected you to be a youth counselor. . . . We'll be sending you an air ticket. . . . Please get your visa sorted out,' I was literally speechless. That was probably the happiest moment of my life."

What the Work Is Like

"The cruise staff members are in charge of all the games, activities, and shore excursions for the passengers. In a way, it's similar to being a camp counselor but for adults. Youth counselors, of course, work with children.

"We make sure the passengers are having fun, and we try to come up with activities and events to capture their interest. We might organize a grandmother's tea or give an origami (paper folding) demonstration or stage a treasure hunt. When in port, we might chaperone a group of passengers on a tour. Even between scheduled activities, we constantly interact and socialize with the passengers."

The Upsides and Downsides

"Working on a cruise ship is my dream job. Every morning I always look forward to getting up and starting the day. I'm not an office person; it's very difficult for me to stay at a desk all day. I've got a lot of energy, and it's great for me being able to move about the ship making lots of friends, being busy.

"The people you work with become like a family. Sometimes you have to share a cabin, and you become very close. Some people worry that working on a cruise ship would be a little like solitary confinement in a prison, that they wouldn't be allowed off of the ship for weeks at a time. But that is hardly the case. When you arrive in port, you always have an opportunity to go ashore. You can go to the beach, shopping, to nightclubs, discos. There are no days off while you're at sea, but you make up for that when you're in port.

"What I like least is having to watch the clock all day. You have to be on the sports deck by nine, down in the lounge by nine-thirty, getting ready in your cabin to be back up on the deck by ten, and so on. You're on a rigid time schedule.

"You have to be constantly energetic and cheerful, even when you don't feel like it. You could work up to fifteen hours a day, but what else are you going to do? The alternative is sitting in your cabin."

Advice from Beverley Citron

"A lot of people give up too easily. They apply once or twice then get discouraged. I sent my resume out to thirty-six cruise lines every three months. For me it took a couple of years and a lot of patience. And over time, I perfected skills that I could add to my resume. Eventually, it paid off. You have to be persistent."

Recommended Reading

How to Get a Job with a Cruise Line, by Mary Fallon Miller. Ticket to Adventure Publishing, P.O. Box 41005, St. Petersburg, FL 33743. Includes descriptions of all the various jobs, an inside look at the different cruise lines, interviews with cruise personnel, and valuable tips on how to go about getting a job.

CHAPTER SEVEN

Water Safety and Rescue

O ur oceans, lakes, rivers, canals, ponds, and swimming pools are a magnet for people who enjoy water sports and recreation. But where there's water, there's also a need for water safety—and, more often than not, water rescue. The U.S. Coast Guard tells us that more than 95 percent of all boating fatalities are from drowning, and more than 90 percent of the victims were not wearing life vests. In more than 70 percent of the incidents, alcohol was involved.

Aquatic types with good physical stamina and the desire to be trained and make a commitment to this type of work can find employment in a variety of settings. They include but are not limited to:

Camps—day and resident (overnight)

Red Cross facilities

Community centers

City and county parks and recreation departments

National parks

YMCA/YWCAs

Jewish community centers

Private country clubs

Apartment complexes

Health clubs

Athletic clubs

Cruise ships

Theme parks and tourist attractions

Yacht Clubs

Possible Job Titles

There are several different job titles—and responsibilities—for those involved with water safety and rescue. Here are just a few:

Lifeguard

National Park Ranger

Firefighter

Paramedic

Emergency Medical Technician

Police Officer

Coast Guard Personnel (a variety of ranks—see Chapter 3)

Navy Personnel (a variety of ranks—see Chapter 3)

Diver

Salvage Diver

In addition, several positions such as swim instructor, swim coach, and boating instructor require safety skills as part of the job. You will learn more about these types of positions in Chapter 8.

The Training You'll Need

The type of training you'll need depends largely upon the setting in which you prefer to work. A camp or recreation center lifeguard will need to learn basic CPR and lifesaving techniques. A firefighter/paramedic, a National Park ranger, or a rescue diver will have a much more intensive training program and will be able to respond to a variety of rescue situations. Of the settings listed above, we will examine in detail three employers of water safety and rescue personnel: camps, the National Park Service, and fire/rescue departments.

Camps

Approximately 6,200 of America's 8,500 summer camps, both resident and day camps, are sponsored or run by social service agencies and nonprofit groups such as the YMCA/YWCA, Boy Scouts of America, Girl Scouts of the USA, religious organizations, and Camp Fire Boys & Girls. Others are operated by school systems or are privately owned.

Camps can be day or resident. Trip camping offers programs in which groups move from site to site, whether by their own power or a utilizing a vehicle or animal, such as horses, bicycles, canoes, or sailboats.

Each summer approximately 500,000 jobs are filled by high school and college students, teachers, doctors, nurses, food service staff and directors, sports specialists, and waterfront instructors and safety professionals. (You will find more information on water sports and waterfront instructors in Chapter 8.)

Most camps begin their summer seasons in late May or June and run until the middle or end of August. Few camps are open after Labor Day.

Camp Waterfront Staff

Whether situated lakeside or by a pool or even at the ocean, most day and resident camps prominently feature waterfront activities, including swim instruction, water safety, and sometimes boating as a cornerstone of their summer programs.

While many specialty camp jobs do not require specific certification, waterfront jobs usually do. Although waterfront activities can often offer the most pleasure—what could be nicer than jumping into a refreshing spring-fed lake to cool off during a hot summer day?—they can also present the most danger. Waterfront staff must be skilled, observant supervisors and well versed in safety procedures, lifesaving and rescue techniques, as well as first aid. Information on finding jobs in camps is provided in Chapter 8.

Training for Waterfront Staff

Camps seeking to hire swimming and boating instructors and lifeguards often expect their staff members to show proof of professional training and will generally want them to possess Red Cross certification.

Here is a sampling of some of the Red Cross courses that lead to that certification.

American Red Cross Lifeguard Certification Course

Purpose: Teach lifeguards the skills and knowledge needed to prevent and respond to aquatic emergencies.

Includes: Adult, child, and infant CPR; CPR for Professional Rescuer; and First Aid Certification. Must be fifteen years of age and attend every session.

Learning objectives: Learn how to understand the value of behaving in a professional manner. Learn how to recognize the characteristic behaviors of distressed swimmers, as well as active and passive drowning victims. Learn to recognize an aquatic emergency and act promptly and appropriately. Learn how to perform equipment-based rescue skills and techniques used by professional lifeguards. Learn how to recognize and care for a possible spinal injury. Learn how to provide first aid and CPR.

Prerequisites: Must be able to swim five hundred yards—one hundred yards each of the front crawl, breaststroke, and sidestroke. (The strokes used for the remaining two hundred yards are the participant's choice.) Tread water for two minutes using legs only, crossing arms across the chest. Submerge to a minimum depth of seven feet, retrieve a ten-pound object, and return to the surface.

Certification requirements: Successfully complete two written exams with a minimum score of 80 percent; complete two final skill scenarios; perform all critical skills.

Course length: Suggested minimum is thirty-three hours (plus a 1.5-hour precourse session).

Certificate validity: Lifeguard Training (including first aid), three years; CPR for the Professional Rescuer, one year.

Red Cross Safety Training for Swim Coaches

Purpose: Provide training in aquatic safety for competitive swim coaches and officials, athletic trainers, athletes participating in aquatic activities, aquatic exercise trainers, and others involved in aquatic competition or exercise programs.

Prerequisites: None.

Learning objectives: Learn to understand the safety responsibilities of an aquatic leader. Learn to recognize hazards associated with swimming pools and explain how to eliminate or minimize these hazards. Learn to recognize a swimmer in distress or drowning. Explain and demonstrate rescue skills. Recognize specific medical conditions that pertain to swimmers. Learn to explain and demonstrate in-line stabilization skills for spinal injury management.

Course length: Suggested minimum is eight hours.

Certification requirements: Successfully complete final skills test and pass written test with a minimum score of 80 percent.

Certificate validity: Three years.

Close-Up

Rose Elizabeth Ledbetter, Lifeguard

Rose Elizabeth Ledbetter worked for two years as a camp lifeguard. She is currently a student at Jacksonville State University in Alabama, working toward a B.A. in English.

"I worked all through my high school and several college summers at camp. I began as a kitchen worker, then moved on to counselor, then I ran a concession, then the last two years I worked as a lifeguard. The camp began as a Baptist camp then was opened for all children, and, the last two years I was there, it was home to Camp Smile-a-Mile, a camp for children who have cancer or have survived it.

"As a lifeguard, things were a little more relaxed than with other positions I had held. The chlorine had to be tested first thing in the morning, but that only took one person, so we took turns. One of us got up at 6:30 A.M., threw on a suit, tested the levels, and added chlorine. The rest of us slept in.

"We weren't required to show up at breakfast, so we usually slept in until ten or fifteen minutes before the first group of campers hit the pool at nine. Then we'd get up, skip the shower, and put on a suit. The style we adopted was a baseball cap with our hair sticking out the back, a tank style suit with a sports bra underneath it, and a pair of oversized men's boxer shorts over the suit with the waist rolled down. The one 'must' was a hat. Even those of us with the darkest complexions needed a hat. I'd always thought my fair skin didn't tan, but even with layers of sunscreen, after a few monster burns I got the tan of a lifetime.

"In the mornings we usually snuck in the kitchen and sweet-talked the staff there into a few leftover breakfast tidbits and then headed down to the pool. After a quick dip to wake ourselves up, we got ready for the campers.

"At the beginning of the season when the campers first arrived at camp, we made them form a single file line at the gate and then directed them to walk in quietly and sit at the edge of the pool. We gave them the rules of the pool: no horseplay, no running, no diving in the shallow end of the pool, no hanging on the rope, no pushing, no hanging on the lifeguard chair.

"We used the buddy system, pairing up the children (an abhorrent system that doesn't work and always leaves one poor kid without a buddy). One of us climbed up into the chair, and the other lined up those who wanted to take the swim test. The test was to swim the length of the pool on the deep side of the rope. That was pretty funny. You wouldn't believe the kids who lied about their swimming abilities to stay with their friends. We also made the counselors take the test after one too many 'grown-ups' lied about their abilities as well.

"Then we sat there looking cool in our shades, swinging our whistles off the ends of our fingers, and watching the campers swim.

"On 'Baywatch,' they save three or four people on every show, but the truth is not nearly so exciting. We made only a save or two a week, and most of those were really more panic than drowning. My first real save was a chaperone who'd had a heart attack in the pool. In all of the lifeguarding classes and the CPR classes I'd taken, no one had informed me that a drowning victim could throw up in your mouth when you gave them mouth to mouth. It was so gross. I wasn't scared when it was going on, but, after everything was OK and the ambulance had left, I walked out of the fence to a clump of bushes and got sick myself. I did that every time.

"In between scheduled swims, we cleaned the pool. Remember this isn't a home pool. The pool was nearly Olympic-size, and the deep end was ten feet. So, to clean the pool, we'd throw in a folding metal chair, balance ourselves standing on the back of the chair with our noses barely poking out of the water, and use a brush to reach the bottom. The sides could be cleaned from out of the water, but cleaning the bottom was a miserable job. A person can get hypothermia even in eighty-degree water in less than an hour. So we were careful to work in short shifts. Still, the work was exhausting and freezing.

"The last group of campers ended their swim times before dinner, and after dinner the pool was open to staffers and chaperones only. Those were the real fun times. We broke every rule we made the kids follow."

Advice from Rose Elizabeth Ledbetter

"Get in shape before camp begins and make sure you get your certification before summer starts.

"To get your lifeguarding license, you have to be sixteen or eighteen, depending on your state. Only two organizations can give you that license: the Red Cross and the YMCA. Classes cost less than $100, but are tough and time-consuming.

"You will be required to know the breaststroke, backstroke, and the sidestroke (lifesaving stroke) and swim these strokes in timed laps.

"You must be able to swim a certain distance, usually the length of the pool, underwater. You must learn several holds and carries as well as different ways to enter and exit the water.

"You must be able to do the dead man's float for a half hour (lifting your face to breathe as needed) and tread water fully clothed for ten to twenty minutes.

"Even if you are not a lifeguard, many camps require that all staffers know CPR and take a basic first aid course. Some camps offer these classes as a seminar for staffers at the beginning of the summer.

"Working at a camp also looks great on a resume. The job instills more responsibility than running a drive through or cooking fries. Some camps take counselors on a volunteer basis. When Smile-a-Mile, a program for young cancer victims, came to our camp, I was a lifeguard. Most of the counselors worked for little or no pay. The experience was well worth it. Contact the local children's hospital if you are interested in this sort of work. Many have summer programs like the one I saw."

Fire and Rescue Departments

Firefighting is no longer the only task assigned to fire departments. Because most fire departments combine fire with rescue service, calls come in that can involve anything from pulling children out of wrecked cars, containing dangerous chemicals that have spilled and are threatening lives or the environment, and performing underwater rescue activities when an occupied car goes off the road and ends up submerged in water.

Underwater rescue teams are trained to dive in the ocean, in lakes, and into dark canals. They know how to operate with zero visibility, feeling their way along the bottom with their hands, searching for a submerged car or body.

But firefighters have to be prepared to handle any type of call. Most firefighters are cross trained. That means that in addition to being firefighters, they have other skills important to fire and rescue service. Cross training helps the fire department get as much of the crew involved in an emergency as needed. For example, firefighters can extricate victims trapped in a car wreck or perform high-angle rescue, rappelling off the top of a building.

Every emergency requires specific skills. Firefighters don't want to arrive at a scene and discover there's no one there to handle a certain problem.

Cross training is also more cost-effective for the fire department and the taxpayers and is certainly more interesting for all
of the firefighters.

Becoming a Firefighter

Gone are the days when a kid fresh out of high school could walk
in the door and say, "Here I am, how 'bout a job?" In the past,
fire departments would take you on and train you. The pay was
low then, and it was dangerous work so not that many people
wanted to become firefighters. These days there is much more
competition, and most fire departments expect you to have
undergone training before you even apply for a job.

If you're serious about working as a firefighter, the best way is
to get some training first. You can take a twelve-week firefighter
training program or study in a two-year program for an associate's degree in fire science.

Once hired, firefighters continue their training, either on
their own or through in-house classes. All skills have to be kept
current, and there are also many specialties to learn.

It is also wise to have good verbal and written skills. Firefighters are often called on to speak in front of groups, and they must
also know how to write reports. Math and chemistry are important too, and those who want to climb the administrative ladder
should also take business and management courses.

But academics are only one part of it. Firefighters must also
have physical and emotional strength. They wear heavy gear and
carry heavy equipment—and regularly run across upsetting situations. Being able to cope is a necessity.

To further enhance your employability, it's a good idea to try
to get some related experience first. Volunteer fire departments
still make up a large percentage of our country's firefighting
force. They usually will accept trainees who are still in school.
The Boy Scouts of America also has a program to train future

firefighters. You can learn more about that at the end of this chapter.

To get a good idea about what firefighting exams are like, you can take a look at the following book at your local library: *Arco Firefighter,* by Robert Andriuolo, Deputy Chief, New York City Fire Department (Prentice Hall).

This book will help prepare you for the different firefighter exams. It reviews the subject matter you'll need to know, provides sample written and physical fitness tests, and gives tips and strategies for earning high test scores.

Becoming a Specialist

Once on the force, you have a number of options open to you. To get on a specialist team—underwater rescue, hazardous materials, and so forth—you first have to exhibit a desire to do the work. Then there has to be an opening on a particular team. But even more important, the team has to feel you would make a good addition. Members would have to trust you and have confidence in your ability to learn.

In addition, each team would require certain training or skills. For example, underwater rescue experts are trained as certified divers. They have to be expert swimmers first, with strength and endurance. In addition to the skills every scuba diver learns, underwater rescue divers must know how to work in pitch-black conditions, in freezing water, or in dangerous rapids or heavy surf conditions. They must also be familiar with various equipment such as grappling hooks or inflatable boats.

Specialist firefighters are a part of the regular combat firefighting team. An underwater rescue specialist, for example, does not wait for a drowning accident before he goes out on a call. He or she is prepared, just as every firefighter is, to answer whatever calls come into the station.

Becoming an EMT

Because fire departments provide so many services in addition to firefighting, most require their force to be EMTs or paramedics.

Emergency medical technicians, or EMTs as they are commonly called, are versed in the basics of first aid and lifesaving.

They learn CPR, patient handling, extrication, and the basics of medical illnesses and medical injuries.

Essentially, EMTs provide basic life support. They're expected to arrive on the scene and take care of a patient until the paramedics get there. If the EMTs and paramedics arrive together, then the EMT assists the paramedic.

If the EMT is working in an area of the country where higher-level paramedics are not a part of the team, he or she is then responsible for getting the patient to the hospital. An EMT might also be responsible for driving the ambulance. In addition to firefighting EMTs, EMTs also work for private ambulance companies and in emergency rooms in some hospitals.

Becoming a Paramedic

Paramedics have to be EMTs before becoming paramedics. Paramedics are trained in very sophisticated, advanced levels of life support. Their goal is to keep a patient alive, and they function in the field as an extension to a physician. They are the pre-hospital hands, eyes, and ears of the doctor and have to be able to assess a situation and react the way a doctor would.

When possible, paramedics contact the hospital and let the doctor know what they've done for the patient. Some ambulances or rescue trucks are capable of transmitting medical data such as electrocardiograms (EKGs) by radio to the hospital. At this point, the doctor can let the paramedics know if there is anything else that should be done before bringing in the patient.

Paramedics have a strong relationship with physicians, who have learned over time to trust the paramedics' training and expertise.

In addition to fire departments, paramedics also work with city or county agencies, for hospitals, and for private ambulance companies.

Training for EMTs and Paramedics

EMTs can generally be trained in six to twelve weeks through a community college. During the course of the program, they spend time observing in hospitals and gaining practical experience riding in an ambulance.

To become certified, EMTs are given a practical exam through the school and a written exam through the state.

Once you have become a certified EMT, you can then go on to paramedic school. Most programs are offered through community colleges, and that is the most popular route to go, though there are a few private paramedic training schools here and there. The training for a paramedic could take anywhere from two or three semesters to two years, depending upon the state in which you live.

The course of study for a paramedic is a full curriculum with course work including anatomy, physiology, pharmacology, the administration and interpretation of EKGs, medical diagnoses, handling cardiac arrests, defibrillation, and all the related medical subjects.

Paramedic trainees spend a lot of time in hospitals learning advanced techniques. They work in operating rooms with anesthesiologists learning intubation, the process of inserting a tube into a patient's windpipe. They also spend time on hospital critical care floors, learning from the nurses how to take care of patients. In addition, trainees also participate in birthings and learn about pediatrics.

Both firefighting EMTs and paramedics learn about the different lifesaving equipment available to them, including extrication devices, air splints, pediatric immobilizers, suction units, and portable defibrillating and EKG machines.

Salaries for EMTs and Paramedics

Depending upon the region of the country, EMTs working for a private ambulance company in a small town can make as low as $5 to $10 an hour. In the dual role of firefighter and EMT, they can make anywhere from $25,000 to $38,000 a year, again depending upon the area of the country. Those figures can rise substantially over the years as experience increases.

Paramedics working independently of a fire department could make anywhere from $12,000 to $20,000 a year. Combined paramedic/firefighters generally start in the mid to high twenties or even in the thirties or low forties in some high-cost cities, and their salaries can go as high as $50,000 or more per year.

For additional information on salaries and hours of work for firefighters in various cities, see the *Municipal Yearbook,* published by the International City Management Association. The yearbook is available in most libraries.

Getting a Head Start

If you are in high school or know someone who is, the Boy Scouts of America has a program for young people to learn about careers in firefighting. Through the Exploring Program, local fire departments work with teens, provide them with uniforms, and teach them the basics of firefighting.

Once each week they meet as a group with professional firefighters who are coordinating the program. They get general training in first aid, the fire trucks, and equipment. After they put in a certain number of hours and are tested, they are allowed to ride on the trucks. They are issued fire gear and can go to fires and other emergencies.

Although cadets are not allowed to go into burning buildings, the program is an excellent way to find out what it's really like being a firefighter.

Cadets can start the program at age fourteen and stay in until they are twenty years old. Cadets often get hired as full-time firefighters right out of the program. Administrators get a chance to see the cadet's work ethic, whether he or she is punctual and responsible, and how a cadet interacts well with other people. The program is open to both girls and boys.

The best way to find out about the Exploring Program in your area is to call your local Boy Scouts Council. The number will be in the telephone directory. For general information you can write the national office at

Boy Scouts of America
Exploring Program
P.O. Box 152079
Irving, TX 75015

Close-Up

Lieutenant Woodrow "Woody" Poitier, Paramedic/Firefighter

Woody Poitier (yes, he is related to the famous actor, Sidney Poitier) became a paramedic first before becoming a firefighter. In fact, he was in the first group of twelve—affectionately called the Dirty Dozen—his city in South Florida hired when its paramedic program was started in 1975.

What the Work Is Like

"My main duty is to preserve life and limb. Whenever we're called for an emergency, we get out and try to take care of the problem. Every call is different.

"I also function as a paramedic supervisor. The paramedic supervisor only goes on certain calls, normally those that involve trauma or calls involving children. That's not to bust anybody's chops, but just to make sure the job is done properly.

"In addition to the emergency calls, there are the reports we have to write, and we also have to stock the truck and make sure the equipment is always ready to go. Every day there's an assignment to take care of.

"We also have controlled drugs on the trucks such as Valium and morphine, and we have to be very careful about that.

"I've delivered about a total of fourteen babies, most of them in the back of ambulances on the interstate. One lady named her child after me.

"I've worked shootings, stabbings, cuttings, drownings, you name it. You get the drunk drivers who cause so many accidents, but most of the time they don't even get hurt. The Lord takes care of children, fools, and drunks. Children are resilient. Even if they get hurt, they seem to have the ability to jump right back.

"I've seen calls where everything has gone right, we have dynamite paramedics on the scene, yet you can't save the victim. Then other times, everything seems to go wrong; you can't get an IV started, nothing seems to be working, and yet he lives.

"There's no rhyme or reason. I do know the paramedics do a good job. Even if you are able to help only one person in a twenty-four-hour period, it makes it worth it.

"It's satisfying work. I really do enjoy being a paramedic. After all these years I'm still gung ho. Even when I'm off duty and I'm at home and hear the sirens go by, it gets the adrenalin going.

"I like most being able to help people. Every emergency is different, and, believe it or not, you come into people's homes, their lives, and the positive energy you input always seems to have a positive result, and that's really, really rewarding.

"But then there are times when you're down, if a child has died for example, but you take the good with the bad.

"Also, we go out on a lot of calls, and most of them are legit-imate calls, but a lot of them are not. These are calls we don't deem as emergency calls. Like the guy who's had a toothache for three days, and he decides to call you at three o'clock in the morning because he can't fall asleep, and he wants you to do something. Or the guy who stubbed his toe. Some people feel that if they call us and go to the hospital on a stretcher they'll get treated more quickly in the emergency room. There's a lot of misuse of the system. But when you get the legitimate calls it makes it all worthwhile."

Advice from Woody Poitier

"If you want a rewarding job and one that actually helps people, then this is the job to go into. But you have to stay in school and get that piece of paper.

"And of course it would help to have some sort of desire to go into the medical field. If you don't want to go to great lengths to become a doctor, the paramedic field would be the way to do it."

National Park Service

The National Park Service, a bureau under the U.S. Department of the Interior, administers more than 350 sites. These encom-pass natural and recreational areas across the country, including the Grand Canyon, Yellowstone National Park, and Lake Mead.

Because most sites are not located near major cities, serious candidates must, for the most part, be prepared to relocate. Housing may or may not be provided, depending upon the site and your position.

Park Rangers

The National Park Service hires three categories of park rangers (generally on a seasonal basis): enforcement, general, and interpretation. Duties vary greatly from position to position and site to site, but rangers in the general division are usually responsible for forestry or resource management; developing and presenting programs that explain a park's historic, cultural, or archeological features; campground maintenance; firefighting; lifeguarding; law enforcement; and performing search-and-rescue activities.

Rangers also sit at information desks, provide visitor services, or participate in conservation or restoration projects. Entry-level employees might also collect fees, provide first aid, and operate audiovisual equipment.

Qualifications and Salaries

In determining a candidate's eligibility for employment and at which salary level he or she would be placed, the National Park Service weighs several factors. In essence, those with the least experience or education will begin at the lowest federal government salary grade of GS-2. But the requirements for that grade are only six months of experience in related work or a high school diploma or its equivalency.

The more related work experience or education, the higher the salary level. For example, GS-4 requires eighteen months of general experience in park operations or in related fields and six months of specialized experience, or one ninety-day season as a seasonal park ranger at the GS-3 level.

Completion of two academic years of college may be substituted for experience if the course work covered is related.

Getting Your Foot in the Door

Competition for jobs, especially at the most well-known sites, can be fierce. But the National Park Service employs a huge permanent staff, and this is supplemented tenfold by an essential seasonal work force during peak visitation periods.

The best way for a newcomer to break in is to start off with seasonal employment during school breaks. With a couple of summer seasons under your belt, the doors will open more easily for permanent employment.

Because of Office of Personnel Management regulations, veterans of the U.S. armed forces have a decided advantage. Depending upon their experience, they may be given preference among applicants.

How to Apply

Recruitment for summer employment begins September 1 with a January 15 deadline. Some sites, such as Death Valley or Everglades National Park, also have a busy winter season. The winter recruitment period is June 1 through July 15.

Applications for seasonal employment with the National Park service can be obtained through the Office of Personnel Management or by writing to the U.S. Department of the Interior, National Park Service, Seasonal Employment Unit, P.O. Box 37127, Washington, DC 20013.

You might also want to contact one of the ten regional offices of the National Park Service. These addresses are listed in the Appendix.

Close-Up

Randy Justice, National Park Ranger

Randy Justice works for the National Park Service, a division of the U.S. Department of the Interior, at Big South Fork National River and Recreation Area in Tennessee and Kentucky. He earned his B.S. in 1982 at Northern Arizona University in

Flagstaff with a major in recreation resource management. He has also participated in many training programs such as law enforcement, swift-water rescue, and basic boating and seamanship courses offered by the U.S. Coast Guard. He has been working for the park service since 1983.

Randy Justice's Background

"I've spent most of my life in the backcountry. When I got into my teens, I started to listen to news reports of people who got into trouble in a place I had just visited and returned from safely. I also started seeing the damage that was being done to the environment by careless people. I wanted to be involved, doing something about this.

"I started my training in college when I joined the Coconino County Search and Rescue team and learned high-mountain rescue and rappelling techniques. I got my first taste of water rescue at the National Park Service Ranger Academy in 1983 at Santa Rosa Community College in California. We spent several days on the Russian River. The water was forty-three degrees, and we were in number four rapids. Six is considered unrunnable. The Swiftwater Rescue Training course covered approaching and stabilizing a victim in moving water, use of throw bags and rescue boards, swimming in rapids, building and operating a tyeoleon, use of the tripod method for crossing moving water, and rope work and knots associated with swift-water rescue. (I was recertified in 1998.)

"I met my first ranger while I was in college. He was the father of a college roommate and a twenty-year veteran of the National Park Service. I started going to the Grand Canyon to visit with them, and I was hooked.

"After college, I had to start off as a part-time seasonal ranger at Lake Powell in Arizona and Utah. The lake is two hundred miles long with two thousand miles of coastline. Unfortunately, my experience there was all body recoveries. The lake is also six hundred feet deep, and some of its victims are still there.

"After starting as a seasonal park ranger, I eventually took a job as a federal police officer with the Department of Defense at Walter Reed Army Hospital, which granted career-conditional status so that I would be able to compete for permanent government jobs. Once in the National Park Service system, you can compete for positions as they become available. The competition, though, is very intense."

What the Work Is Like

"As a ranger, let me stress that the water rescue is only a small part of my job. The National Park Service is considered one of the most highly trained agencies in the government. I am also a federal police officer, an Emergency Medical Technician, a wildland firefighter, helicopter crew member, self-defense instructor, and DARE officer (Drug Abuse Resistance Education, a program taught only by law enforcement officers).

"Boring is not in a ranger's vocabulary. My day might start at three in the morning with a call from the dispatcher sending me to look for a lost child, go to a car accident, or participate in the rescue of rafters stranded in the river during an unanticipated flood.

"I have been at eight parks in my career, starting with Lake Powell and going to Death Valley, the Grand Canyon, Washington, D.C., Shenandoah, Lowell National Historical Park (outside of Boston), Valley Forge, and presently Big South Fork National River and Recreation Area. Some of the parks had a lot of law enforcement, some a lot of resource management, and Lowell and Big South Fork have had the most water rescues and/or recoveries.

"At Lowell I was on the rescue team at a large kayak competition. Lowell also had five miles of historical canals. These canals were a magnet for the neighborhood kids. In two and a half years, I helped to recover seven bodies; six were preteens. As a DARE officer, I had a chance to bring a water safety message to the young people of the city.

"During the busy season, a forty-hour work week is a rarity, and there are no time clocks. Sixteen-hour days are not unusual. I also go on special details anywhere in the country that can last for twenty-one days. I have provided security for two presidents, a vice president, and several dignitaries.

"Most of my job at Big South Fork is more resource based with a lot of patrol, including running the white water in rafts and kayaks.

"The best part of the job is when I get to make a difference in a young person's life. It may come in the classroom during my DARE class or when I do a bike patrol and wind up with a dozen kids following me on bikes pretending they're rangers. One day I was on patrol in a marked car when I came upon a serious bike accident. One of the bystanders saw me and said, 'There's someone who can help.' That means something to me.

"The downside is watching people make the same mistakes I saw people making fifteen years ago. Even with all the education and communication, I still see people ill prepared, drinking and driving or boating, and young men suffering from machoism.

"No one does this for the money. The federal government pays employees based on a General Services (GS) pay scale. Beginning seasonal rangers usually start at GS-4 or GS-5; most permanent rangers are either GS-7 or GS-9. Right now a GS-9 law enforcement ranger makes $18.99 an hour."

Advice from Randy Justice

"Folks interested in this line of work should know going in that they aren't doing it for the money but instead for the sense of self-accomplishment they get at the end of a hard day. They should also realize that many of the people they rescue or assist won't even acknowledge the work that the rangers have done—they take it for granted that someone will be there to assist them when they get themselves in trouble. Another downside more specifically related to water rescues is that most of the time they turn into body recoveries.

"Wanting to help others, a desire to protect the natural resources of our country, and an interest in the out-of-doors are important traits to have.

"Look for training from the Coast Guard Auxiliary, adult education services, and local colleges. If there's a rescue team in your community, ask to speak with them and see firsthand what is involved before you get in over your head. Physical stamina is important, and many rescue calls will come when least expected. If you aren't willing or able to fully commit to this life, then you should find out before you invest too much in training.

"And remember that keeping yourself safe is as important as helping others. This year I was recertified in swift-water training from the same agency that I was first trained by fifteen years ago; it was tougher this time around!"

CHAPTER EIGHT

Water Sports

That old adage, "those who can, do; those who can't, teach," couldn't be further from the truth when it comes to water sports. To teach swimming, diving, boating, windsurfing, and all the other water sports, instructors first must be proficient in the necessary skill area—and in many cases certified by a particular organization, for example, the Red Cross or the Professional Association of Diving Instructors (PADI).

In Chapter 7, we learned about all the possible places for water safety and rescue. Those same settings afford water fun, too. Those with a water sport skill can become instructors in their areas of expertise. Here are some of the different types of water sports.

Swimming (basic through advanced skills, plus competitive swimming)

Boating (canoeing, kayaking, motor boating, sailing)

Waterskiing

Scuba diving

Snorkeling

Windsurfing

Charter fishing

Charter boating

Job Settings

Adult Education

Most adult and continuing education programs offer water sport instruction, from basic swimming to sailing and diving, and hire experienced instructors to carry out their programs. Consult your local board of education, library, community college, or look in the phone book under adult or continuing education.

Apartment Complexes

Some large apartment complexes with pools hire lifeguards or swim instructors to provide classes to children and adult residents. Most would advertise openings in the local paper or tack up announcements on clubhouse bulletin boards.

Camps

Day and resident summer camps are one of the largest employers of water sport instructors. Typically camps offer swimming and boating—canoeing or sailing—and some camps specialize in a particular activity such as windsurfing or diving.

The best advice camping professionals will give you is to start early to find that job. Many jobs are lined up as much as a year in advance, taken by counselors and other staff members who plan to work every summer for a particular camp.

In the Appendix, you will find a list of national organizations offering camping programs, and they provide listings of camp vacancies upon request. When you make contact with them, be specific about the employment information you are seeking and the geographic location in which you would like to work. Some of these organizations accept resumes and will forward them to local councils.

Colleges and Universities

Many colleges and universities offer physical education majors and need qualified instructors for their various programs. In most cases you will need an advanced degree in physical education or a related field to land a job in a university setting.

Community Centers and Parks and Recreation Departments

Community centers and city and county parks and recreation departments usually offer summer and year-round programs in swim instruction and other water sports. It is not always necessary to wait for a job opening to appear in the local newspaper. Through the phone book, you can find offices near you. A phone call or a resume left at the office can often result in a job.

Country Clubs, Hotels, and Resorts

Country clubs, hotels, and resorts often have pools or lakeside or beachfront property. They may operate boating, diving, and windsurfing schools. Check the local newspaper for job listings or make the rounds in person.

Dive Clubs and Shops

For certified dive instructors, the first place to start your job search would be through local dive shops. They often sponsor diving training and would also know of other organizations in the area offering the same thing.

Health and Athletic Clubs

Many health and athletic clubs offer swim instruction. They also provide coaching for professional athletes or swimmers in training for competition.

Yacht Clubs

Yacht clubs are obvious places to look for positions teaching sailing and other types of boating.

YMCA/YWCAs

The YMCA/YWCA is one of the biggest employers of youth leaders, recreation workers, activity and speciality instructors, and other related positions. Jobs are filled both in YMCA and YWCA city and town centers as well as at a variety of Y-sponsored resident and day camps around the country. Contact your local Y for information on job openings and requirements.

The Training You'll Need

Some employers will not require specific certification to hire you in some positions. If, for example, you can demonstrate that you are a competent windsurfer and have the skills all instructors require—patience, the ability to teach—you might find the job is yours.

On the other hand, some sports such as swimming or diving require extensive training and certification before you can teach. Here are a couple of examples.

Swim Instructors

For information on swim instructor, lifesaving, and lifeguard courses, contact your local Red Cross or YMCA/YWCA.

Red Cross Water Safety Instructor Certificate

Purpose: Train instructor candidates to teach the Infant and Preschool Aquatics Program; the seven levels of the Learn to

Swim Program; the Community Water Safety and Water Safety Instructor Aide courses; and, for eligible individuals, the Safety Training for Swim Coaches course.

Certification requirements: Successfully participate in course activities, meet instructor candidate competencies, and pass a written test with a minimum score of 80 percent.

Prerequisites: Must possess an Instructor Candidate Training certificate issued in the last twelve months or a current Health and Safety Services instructor authorization and successfully complete the precourse session consisting of tests of water safety and swimming skills and knowledge.

Minimum age: Seventeen by end of course.

Learning objectives: Learn to use program materials effectively and to learn to plan and conduct effective courses. Learn to evaluate the progress of students for certification and prepare and submit accurate records and reports.

Course length: Suggested minimum is thirty-six hours (not including the precourse session).

Certification validity: Authorization is for two calendar years. All authorizations expire on December 31.

Diving Instructors

There are four or five nationally and internationally recognized certifying agencies for dive instructors such as Professional Association of Diving Instructors (PADI) and National Association of Underwater Instructors (NAUI). Certified courses in basic diving and then instructor training are offered through colleges and universities, the YMCA/YWCA, adult education, and dive shops. A glance through the phone book will point you in the right direction.

Each certifying body has its own requirements for recognizing the accomplishments of dive instructors. Most require a step progression, from diver to assistant instructor to divemaster to full instructor.

NAUI Instructor Levels

There are several instructor levels offered by NAUI. Here are just two: assistant instructor (AI) and divemaster.

Assistant Instructor

As an AI, you will be authorized to teach all aspects of skin and scuba diving under the supervision of a NAUI instructor. This is the best possible way to develop your instructional skills. The rating can be a step toward full instructor or an end in itself.

The program is designed to introduce students to diving instruction basics. It also tests individuals in fundamental water skills needed to be capable assistants.

Additional training or experience is to be obtained by the assistant instructor who desires to assist in highly specialized training activities, such as deep, wreck penetration, cavern, or ice dives.

Divemaster

An active-status NAUI divemaster, one step below full instructor, is qualified to organize and conduct dives for certified divers if the diving activities and locales approximate those in which the divemaster is trained. Additional training, knowledge, or experience is necessary for the divemaster who desires to organize highly specialized activities, such as wreck penetration, cavern, or ice dives, or to enter a new locale.

An active-status NAUI divemaster is qualified to assist an active-status NAUI instructor in diving courses. If all other prerequisites are met, a current NAUI divemaster is qualified to enter a NAUI Instructor Training Course (ITC). (Attending a NAUI Instructor Preparatory Program [PREP] and NAUI Assistant Instructor certification are recommended prior to attending an ITC.)

Charter Skipper

Not all water sports jobs involve teaching. Charter skippers take passengers out to sea, usually for fishing or diving expeditions but sometimes for snorkeling or sight-seeing. The skipper acts as fishing expert, deckhand, and host.

Lee Woods is a sailing instructor and experienced charter skipper. His profile regarding the former is showcased later in this chapter. Here's what he has to say about being a charter skipper.

What the Work Is Like

"Much of a charter skipper's role is that of a host, and he or she must, therefore, be cordial and able to relate to many different personalities. In some instances, if the boat is large enough, say forty feet or more, the captain might have a helper to work the boat and help serve meals and drinks.

"When there is no captain or crew aboard, when the guests operate the boat themselves, it is called a bareboat charter, although the boat is fully equipped.

"In general, a fishing charter boat captain typically owns his or her own boat, and that is the captain's principal livelihood.

"Many charter skippers often work as staff for charter companies or as freelance charter skippers, much like instructors. And, in most cases, they, too, have a helper who works with them, taking care of the boat and serving meals and drinks.

"Charter skippers can operate at local levels, taking people fishing or just out for a day on the water, then back to the marina, or they can operate for days at a time, weeks sometimes, aboard a large vessel moving from one locale to another."

The Skills You Must Have

"Many good charter skippers bring a variety of skills to their trades. Many speak several languages, and many play musical instruments or are great story tellers. Many crew members have been trained in a variety of cooking skills and preparing drinks.

"The skipper or boat owner must, of course, be expert at keeping the boat and all its systems in proper working order. Skippers and helpers must also be skilled in temporary medical treatment for common problems such as sunburn, cuts, and burns.

"A charter skipper must also know the waters, the cruising grounds he or she will be operating in, and often the little-known anchorages or stop offs that offer some unique attraction. Knowledge of the area's history also helps. Charter guests often have a million questions about where they are, so good skippers will have answers.

"Surveys have shown that no matter how skilled a charter skipper may be in seamanship, boat handling, navigation, and other related skills, they are remembered by charterers for their skills at creating a happy social environment and making others feel at home and secure. So, it is people skills that separate the so-so skippers from those who are sought out by charter guests."

Earnings

"Typical fees are around $100 a day per person, plus meals. Charter guests who read the fine print, or those who are aware of the charter business, know that a 10 percent tip is also part of the package.

"The independents, however, must bear the brunt of the extra expense of promoting their own businesses but also do not have to pay a percentage to a charter company. Many advertise in international magazines and prepare brochures on their boats and cruising grounds."

A Typical Charter

"The skipper will make sure the boat is spotless and that all necessary items are aboard. Charter guests have a variety of options in 'provisioning' the boat, or deciding whether to pay to have the charter company supply food and drink or whether to buy such items as they cruise from location to location. The more a skipper knows about guest preferences, the better the odds of success.

"Next, the skipper works with the charter company to determine what kind of cruise the guests prefer—lazy and slow or on the move, for example. Where do they want to go? What do they want to do? Snorkel? Dive? Sightsee? Do they want one of the company's prepared packages, or do they want to play it by ear? Again, homework is the key to success—finding out anything and everything that will make charter guests go away thinking it was the best vacation they've ever had.

"Like an instructor, a charter skipper must be ever mindful of safety for guests. Many charter guests are not even boaters and are just along for the ride and, therefore, have no idea of what to expect. The skipper must explain fundamental safety measures and keep an eye on passengers at all times.

"Charter guests are typically on vacation and tend to have a few drinks. Alcohol can be a deadly enemy aboard a boat, and the skipper must balance fun with prudence."

Getting Your Captain's License

"The first step any hopeful must take is a bit of self-appraisal. Before any candidates are given permission to take the exam, they must show the Coast Guard that they have had a substantial amount of experience (usually years) on their own or other vessels. If candidates feel they are prepared to carry this kind of license, then they can proceed.

"Next, get in touch with the nearest Coast Guard district office. Any library reference section will have a phone number and address. Call or write and ask for information on getting the license. In a month or so, candidates will receive a stack of forms to fill out, plus a checklist of what to do: documents to gather, physical and eye exams, drug test, and so forth.

"The central ingredient in this package is the sea service form asking candidates to document their experience, including dates at sea and the number of hours. Candidates return the information to the Coast Guard, keeping a copy of everything, and then wait. Usually, within a month, they will receive a yes or no response on whether they will be allowed to take the exam. They will also receive test dates and testing center locations.

"Candidates may have to travel to another city and should plan on staying all day. First-time candidates will be taking the exam for 'master of inland steam/motor or auxiliary sail vessels,' often referred to as the six-pack license. With this entry-level license, captains are permitted to carry no more than six passengers. It is a beginning, but the exam itself is not for beginners in the field. It is difficult by any standard and covers a wide variety of marine topics, including inland and international rules of the road, navigation, fire science, sound and light signals, and relevant federal regulations. The questions have little to do with pleasure boating and more to do with formal merchant marine rules and regulations, boat handling, and seamanship.

"There is no practical component, no on-water testing, much to the satisfaction of many candidates. Candidates who fail are permitted to retake only the failed portions at a later date. All successful candidates receive their licenses in the mail, which must then be renewed every five years, including testimonials that candidates are continuing to work in the field.

"A license is a necessary step in any professional captain's career and will open many doors that might be otherwise closed."

Close-Ups

Claire Best, Swimming Instructor

Claire Best worked as a swim instructor both at a resident Girl Scout camp and for a metropolitan YMCA in New England.

Claire Best's Background

"Between the time I was eight years old and nineteen, I spent almost every summer of my life at a variety of camps, in one capacity or another. I started with day camps, and then at age twelve I was finally allowed to go away to overnight camp. At age fifteen I was made a CIT, Counselor-in-Training, and at age seventeen I got my first paying camp job, as a swim and canoeing instructor at a Girl Scout camp in Maine. Two years later, I was a general counselor at another camp. Even in college I ended up doing similar work in my work-study program, employed by the local YMCA as a swim instructor and also as a youth counselor.

"My years as a camper prepared me for work as a counselor. I had learned a lot of skills, some of which I was later able to help other campers learn. Swimming was my strongest area, and by the time I was sixteen I had passed my Red Cross junior and then senior lifesaver tests. I never did go on for my WSI (Water Safety Instructor), but I was lucky. I was able to find work without it. It helped that at the time the YMCA followed a different swimming program than the Red Cross. These days, though, the more certification you have, the better it is for you."

What the Work Was Like

"As a camp swim instructor I spent all day at the waterfront, on the dock, or in the water, teaching beginner, intermediate, and advanced swimmers. With the little children, you had to be in the water with them, both for their safety and to reassure them as well as to demonstrate.

"The older children who were better swimmers needed less demonstration, so, if you didn't feel like getting wet on a certain day, you could just set them to swimming laps. I'd call out instructions to help them improve their strokes. By the end of the day, my voice would be hoarse, or I'd feel pretty waterlogged sometimes. But it was a great way to spend the summers, in the sun all day."

The Upsides

"Camp life is what I enjoyed the most. The commotion in the dining hall, living in a rustic cabin in a wooded setting, the camp fires at night, the songs, the skits, the sports competitions. And the friendships. They were free and easy days. The salaries were pretty horrendous, but you got room and board and a couple of days off here or there to explore the surrounding area. It was like a paid vacation."

Lee Woods, Sailing Instructor and Charter Skipper

Lee Woods, whom we met earlier in this chapter, is currently on staff with Diamond 99 Marina in Melbourne, Florida, an affiliate of the American Sailing Association and one of approximately one hundred affiliates in the United States, Caribbean, Canada, and Europe. He is a sailing instructor and a charter skipper.

He earned his B.A. in journalism from the University of Miami in 1973, with graduate studies in science communication at Boston School of Public Communications and an MIT summer program in technical writing. He is also a certified instructor in basic sailing, coastal cruising, and coastal navigation. He also has a Coast Guard captain's license.

Lee Woods' Background

"I began in 1970 when I arranged a deal with a sailor friend. I would teach him guitar if he would teach me to sail. From the moment I first saw a sailboat on the water, sails full, leaning slightly, cutting through the water, I was hooked. I had to learn.

"As a self-professed adventurer, this was an adventure I could enjoy in my hometown. It was not my primary field—journalism was—but it became more and more of a goal to incorporate sailing as a source of income. In the beginning, however, it was something that I simply wanted to master.

"At first, my friend tried to teach me the rudiments. It was frustrating, as any new and challenging learning experience is, but I kept practicing on my own, making mistakes and learning little by little. I also hitchhiked with friends when I could and helped them crew their boats.

"In Florida, I signed up for courses at the Indian River Sailing Club in Indian Harbor Beach and remained a part of that group for several years, earning student certifications in several levels of sailing.

"Then, another desire I have always had, teaching, brought me to the ASA's Instructor Certification Clinic in Punta Gorda, Florida, on the Gulf Coast, a rigorous program designed to test and certify instructors. Here, I earned my instructor ratings. Shortly thereafter, in 1988, I took the exam for the Coast Guard captain's license. This license cannot gather dust. It must be renewed every five years, with written proof of work being carried out in the marine industry."

What the Work Is Like

"Like many instructors who teach sports, I soon realized that I had several categories of concentration. First my sailing skills had to be as close to flawless as possible, given the whims of the elements and anyone's occasional goof in an environment that is fundamentally foreign to human beings. After sailing skills, I realized that I had to study the techniques of teaching and working with adults. Too many instructors feel that if they know how to sail they know how to teach. Not so. A good instructor will put as much study into teaching techniques as he or she will into sailing skills. Finally, I had to acknowledge that sailing schools are businesses, with profit and loss just like any other business. There are always insurance issues, personal and training-facility liabilities, and so forth. I also had to promote the school among the students. I had to make sure the training boat was in top shape, that the gear was working, and that everything was ready when the students arrived. I had to remind some students that they hadn't paid the full amount and would have to before we could begin the class. I had to make sure everyone could make each of the sailing dates and, when someone had to miss one, figure out how to make that up.

"The work is exciting, challenging, never boring, and always rewarding. There is a bit of apprehension, of course, as an instructor, in that you don't want to make too many mistakes, and you hope the wind, storms, or unknown circumstances will not put you, the boat, and your students in harm's way. A good instructor will not take beginners into a day of bad weather. Students are often crowded together in a small boat and must deal with a sudden 'social density' that often violates an individual's personal space. Students have an inherent fear of the unknown and what they cannot control and will not learn anything if they are in emotional or physical distress. If they are frightened enough, they may not return for the second lesson.

"A typical first day for, say, basic sailing, would go something like this: you meet and greet the students, let them introduce themselves, talk about the program and what it entails, let them know what to expect, try to ease any fears they may have, and recommend any necessary gear they might need—gloves, boat shoes, and so on.

"Then you introduce them to the boat, explaining the various components and their purposes. Then it's onto the water, with the primary goal of letting the students do the sailing, letting them make mistakes.

"All instructors, at this point, begin to see the various personalities emerging. Some will want to dominate, while others recoil. Like any group endeavor, students come from all walks, all ages, all temperaments, and it is the instructor's job to create a blend and encourage the students to work together. An instructor must also never forget that adults, if they are not having fun, are not going to learn. An instructor must mix humor and relaxation with instruction. There is no room for Captain Bligh or anyone who yells at students. Eventually, instructors discover that they must also examine their own temperaments and abilities to create a harmonious atmosphere where the so-called stupid question does not exist and where everyone gets equal time learning the various methods and techniques.

"On the water, an instructor follows a typical learning format: show, demonstrate, let the students try, then reinforce through repetition, and always compliment their achievements.

"Most basic sailing programs do not last more than twelve hours (three days, four hours each day), so a great deal of learning must take place quickly. At the end of four hours, most students are overwhelmed, excited, thrilled, or scared to death! It is the instructor's role now, at the end of the day, to create what's called a 'looking-back' session, sometimes at a nearby restaurant or at the training facility, where the group can relive the day, talk about concerns, problems, and so on.

"This is a time when the instructor can use sketches or photos or any other training aid to help the students reinforce the learning. In all, if anyone loves to sail, loves to help people learn, the job of a sailing instructor is by far one of the most rewarding jobs anyone could have. Plus, you often get a terrific tan!"

Advice from Lee Woods

"Be a sponge. Learn to sail and learn to sail well. You do not have to be an America's Cup skipper, but you must know the boat inside out and be prepared to handle any situation that might arise. Students will expect you to demonstrate skills and techniques competently. If you cannot, then you are not ready to become an instructor. As in any field, the instructor must know far, far more than he or she ever has to teach.

"Sign up for and take all the programs possible, then continue on into instructor ratings. Eventually, individuals interested in this line of work must take the Coast Guard captain's license exam. Any vessel used for anything other than pleasure must have a licensed captain aboard.

"One mistake many hopefuls make is to try the route of learning from a friend or relative. There are many excellent sailors who are not affiliated with an established program, but established programs do give students accepted, internationally acknowledged methods and techniques, something many lesser prepared individuals cannot offer a beginner. Safety issues, for example, are often ignored when friends teach friends.

"Also, there are many magazines and books that cover the field, both in the library and in bookstores. For sailors, two notable magazines are *Sail* and *Cruising World*, both available on local magazine racks.

"Then, pick the brains of those who know, hang around marinas and get to know people, possibly even people who will take you sailing with them. Many people make their way around the world volunteering as crew members.

"The charter skipper who combines boating skills with those of a host can skipper a small fishing vessel on a lake or act as skipper on a mega-yacht owned by corporations or the wealthy.

"Like tennis or skiing instructors, sailing instructors and charter skippers are, as they say, a dime a dozen. The pay is, therefore, not that much, typically $10 an hour for a freelance sailing instructor. Some yacht skippers earn as much as $50,000 a year, depending on the type and size of the yacht and the enterprise.

"Overall, the life of a sailing instructor or charter skipper is rich in reward, but only when all the homework has been done and only when instructors and skippers themselves continue to learn."

Professional Associations

F or more information on the careers covered in this book, contact the appropriate professional associations listed below. In addition to information and professional contacts, some professional associations offer grants, scholarships, and training opportunities.

Aquatic Science

American Cetacean Society
P.O. Box 1391
San Pedro, CA 90733

American Fisheries Society
5410 Grosvenor Lane, Suite 110
Bethesda, MD 20814

American Geophysical Union
2000 Florida Avenue NW
Washington, DC 20009

American Society of Limnology and Oceanography
Great Lakes Research Division
University of Michigan
Ann Arbor, MI 48109

American Society of Mammalogists
Virginia Museum of Natural History
1001 Douglas Avenue
Martinsville, VA 24112

Send a self-addressed stamped envelope with 5.25-inch or 3.5-inch, IBM-compatible, formatted disc to receive a list of grant sources.

American Society of Mammalogists
Institute of Ecosystem Studies
Box AB
Millbrook, NY 12545

Grants-in-Aid of Research, up to $1,000 are open to graduate students and upper-level undergraduates who are members of the American Society of Mammalogists. Annual application deadline in March of each year. Albert R. and Alma Shadle Fellowship in mammalogy: applicants must be United States citizens and enrolled in or accepted for a graduate program in mammalogy in a U.S. college or university.

American Society of Mammalogists
Secretary-Treasurer
501 Widtsoe Building
Brigham Young University
Provo, UT 84602

American Veterinary Medical Association
1931 North Mecham Road, Suite 1000
Schaumburg, IL 60173

American Zoo and Aquarium Association
Executive Office and Conservation Center
7970-D Old Georgetown Road
Bethesda, MD 20814

American Zoo and Aquarium Association
Office of Membership Services
Oglebay Park
Wheeling, WV 26003

Consortium of Aquariums, Universities, and Zoos
Department of Psychology
California State University
Northridge, CA 91330

Environmental Careers Organization
286 Congress Street
Boston, MA 02210

European Association for Aquatic Mammals
Secretary/Treasurer
Postbus 58
3910 AB Rhenen, The Netherlands

European Cetacean Society
Dr. Harald Benke
Deutches Museum fur Meereskunde und Fischerei
Katharinenberg 14-20
D-18439 Stralsund, Germany

Gulf Coast Research Laboratory
Scott Marine Education Center
P.O. Box 7000
Ocean Springs, MS 39564

International Association for Aquatic Animal Medicine
Department of Fish & Wildlife Resources
College of Forestry, Wildlife, and Range Sciences
University of Idaho
Moscow, ID 83844

International Marine Animal Trainers Association
1200 South Lake Shore Drive
Chicago, IL 60605

International Oceanographic Foundation
4600 Rickenbacker Causeway
Miami, FL 33149

Marine Technology Society
1825 K Street NW
Washington, DC 20006

Minority Institutions
Marine Science Association
Biology Department, Box 18540
Jackson State University
Jackson, MS 39217

National Oceanic & Atmospheric Administration
Marine Policy Fellowships
National Sea Grant College Program
1335 East-West Highway
Silver Spring, MD 20910

Oceanic Engineering Society
Institute of Electrical and Electronics Engineers
345 East Forty-seventh Street
New York, NY 10017

The Oceanography Society
1755 Massachusetts Avenue NW, Suite 700
Washington, DC 20036

The Society for Marine Mammalogy
School of Fisheries WH10/U
University of Washington
Seattle, WA 98195

Student Conservation Association
Resource Assistant Program
Earth Work
Department EW, Box 550
Charlestown, NH 03603

Technical Committee on Acoustical Oceanography
Acoustical Society of America
500 Sunnyside Boulevard
Woodbury, NY 11797

Women's Aquatic Network
P.O. Box 4993
Washington, DC 20008

Navy and Coast Guard

Each of the military services publishes handbooks, fact sheets, and pamphlets describing entrance requirements, training and advancement opportunities, and other aspects of military careers. These publications are widely available at all recruiting stations, most state employment service offices, and in high schools, colleges, and public libraries.

Commercial Fishing

For general information about fishing occupations, contact

National Fisheries Institute
1525 Wilson Boulevard, Suite 500
Arlington, VA 22209

For information on licensing requirements to fish in a particular area, contact

National Marine Fisheries Service
NMFS Scientific Publications Office
7600 Sand Point Way NE
Seattle, WA 98115

Names of postsecondary schools offering fishing and related marine educational programs are available from

Marine Technology Society
1828 L Street NW, Suite 906
Washington, DC 20036

Information about licensing of fishing vessel captains and mates—and requirements for merchant mariner documentation—is available from the U.S. Coast Guard Marine Inspection Office or Marine Safety Office in your state or

Licensing and Evaluation Branch
U.S. Coast Guard
2100 Second Street SW
Washington, DC 20593

For information about certified training programs for diving (umbilical) careers, contact

College of Oceaneering
272 South Fries Avenue
Wilmington, CA 90744

Water Transportation

Information on merchant marine careers, training, and licensing requirements is available from

Maritime Administration
U.S. Department of Transportation
400 Seventh Street SW, Room 302
Washington, DC 20590

U.S. Coast Guard
Licensing and Manning Compliance Division (C-MOC-1)
2100 Second Street SW
Washington, DC 20593

Individuals who are interested in attending a merchant marine academy should contact

Admissions Office
U.S. Merchant Marine Academy
Steamboat Road
Kings Point, NY 11024

Cruise Staff

Cruise Line International Association
500 Fifth Avenue, Suite 1407
New York, NY 10110

Water Safety

For information on water safety courses and first aid and CPR, contact local chapters of the American Red Cross or its national headquarters at

American Red Cross
National Headquarters
Seventeenth & D Streets NW
Washington, DC 20006

For information on careers with the YMCA, contact

YMCA of the USA
101 North Wacker Drive
Chicago, IL 60606

General information about emergency medical technicians and paramedics is available from

National Association of Emergency Medical Technicians
9140 Ward Parkway
Kansas City, MO 64114

Information concerning training courses, registration, and job opportunities can be obtained by writing to the State Emergency Medical Service Director, listed in your phone book.

For information on careers in firefighting, contact

International Association of Fire Fighters
1750 New York Avenue NW
Washington, DC 20006

For information about employment with the National Park Service, contact

U.S. Department of the Interior
National Park Service
P.O. Box 37127
Washington, DC 20013

You may also contact one of the ten regional offices of the National Park Service.

Alaska Region
National Park Service
2525 Gambell Street
Anchorage, AK 99503

Midwest Region
National Park Service
1709 Jackson Street
Omaha, NE 68102

Pacific Northwest Region
National Park Service
83 South King Street, #212
Seattle, WA 98104

Southeast Region
National Park Service
75 Spring Street SW
Atlanta, GA 30303

Western Region
National Park Service
600 Harrison Street, #600
San Francisco, CA 94107

Mid-Atlantic Region
National Park Service
143 South Third Street
Philadelphia, PA 19106

Rocky Mountain Region
National Park Service
P.O. Box 25287
Denver, CO 80225

National Capital Region
National Park Service
1100 Ohio Drive SW
Washington, DC 20242

Southwest Region
National Park Service
P.O. Box 728
Santa Fe, NM 87501

North Atlantic Region
National Park Service
15 State Street
Boston, MA 02109

Water Sports

For information on careers in camping and summer counselor opportunities, contact

American Camping Association
5000 State Road 67 North
Martinsville, IN 46151

For information on careers with the YMCA, contact

YMCA of the USA
101 North Wacker Drive
Chicago, IL 60606

For information on camping jobs and openings, contact the following organizations:

4-H Extension Service
3860 South Building USDA
Washington, DC 20250

Boys and Girls Clubs of America
771 First Avenue
New York, NY 10017

Boy Scouts of America
1325 Walnut Hill Lane
P.O. Box 152079
Irving, TX 75015

Camp Fire Boys and Girls, Inc.
4601 Madison Avenue
Kansas City, MO 64110

Christian Camping International
P.O. Box 646
Wheaton, IL 60189

Girl Scouts of USA
420 Fifth Avenue
New York, NY 10018

Jewish Welfare Board
15 East Twenty-sixth Street
New York, NY 10016

Information about sport or recreational fishing occupations is available from

Sport Fishing Institute
1010 Massachusetts Avenue NW
Washington, DC 20001

For information on local government jobs in recreation, con-tact the nearest department of parks and recreation.

For information on positions available in recreation and parks departments, contact

National Recreation and Park Association
Division of Professional Services
2775 South Quincy Street, Suite 300
Arlington, VA 22206

For information on careers in employee services and recre-ation, contact

The American Association for Leisure and Recreation (AALR)
1900 Association Drive
Reston, VA 22091

National Employee Services and Recreation Association
2211 York Road, Suite 207
Oakbrook, IL 60521

For more information about how to become a diving instructor, contact

NAUI Worldwide
9942 Currie Davis Drive, Suite H
Tampa, FL 33619
Website: www.padi.com

For information on how to pursue a career as a sailing instructor, contact

American Sailing Association (ASA)
13922 Marquesas Way
Marina del Ray, CA 90292

About the Author

A full-time writer of career books, Blythe Camenson works hard to help job seekers make educated choices. She firmly believes that with enough information, readers can find long-term, satisfying careers. To that end, she researches traditional as well as unusual occupations, talking to a variety of professionals about what their jobs are really like. In all of her books she includes firsthand accounts from people who reveal what to expect in each occupation.

Camenson was educated in Boston, earning her B.A. in English and psychology from the University of Massachusetts and her M.Ed. in counseling from Northeastern University.

In addition to *Careers for Aquatic Types & Others Who Want to Make a Splash*, she has written more than three dozen books for NTC/Contemporary Publishing Group, Inc.